Church Worth Getting Up For

Charles E. Gutenson

Abingdon Press
Nashville

CHURCH WORTH GETTING UP FOR

Copyright © 2013 Charles E. Gutenson

This book is printed on acid-free paper.

Library of Congress Cataloging-in-Publication Data

Gutenson, Charles E.
  Church worth getting up for / Charles E. Gutenson.
      pages cm
  Includes bibliographical references.
  ISBN 978-1-4267-5775-4 (pbk. : alk. paper) 1. Church attendance. 2. Church. I. Title.
  BV652.5.G88 2013
  254'.5—dc23
                              2013006853

13 14 15 16 17 18 19 20 21 22—10 9 8 7 6 5 4 3 2 1

MANUFACTURED IN THE UNITED STATES OF AMERICA

To Beulah Walker Applegate,
as fine a mother-in-law as a man could want

CONTENTS

INTRODUCTION

Over the course of the last few years, I have found myself traveling often and, consequently, attending different churches. Sometimes my wife has been with me, sometimes not. Too often, though, I have found myself either asking her or saying to myself, "If I were not already a Christian, why would I have gotten out of bed to come to this?" I don't mean to be as critical as it might sound on first blush, although I'll admit, I have attended some very disappointing church services. Instead, I was trying to put myself in the position of that growing percentage of our population that finds church no longer worth getting up for. If I, a lifelong Christian, was having a hard time finding myself engaged, encouraged, or challenged, then is it any wonder that those not already followers of Jesus would find church largely boring and irrelevant?

So, the question for me, as a person for whom giving up on the church is not an option, quickly ceased being "Why would I get up?" and became "What would make it *worth* getting up for?" What are the factors that are either keeping folks away from church or driving away those who had been regulars? We are painfully aware that for some time, studies have shown decline in church attendance as well as decline in the number of Americans who self-identify as Christians. In fact, given the level of decline among the group under 35, one cannot help being seriously concerned about the future of the church in America. It is to this set of questions and concerns that this book is committed.

1

Far too often, I fear, the answers we give to these challenges end up being self-serving. Why do folks avoid coming to church? Well, so we say, it is because we preach about sinful behaviors and folks don't want to hear about that. They want to be affirmed in the midst of their behaviors, so they stay away from church. Except, of course, numerous studies conducted over quite a span of years by noted pollster George Barna have demonstrated that self-identified, born-again Christians really behave, for all practical purposes, no differently than the culture at large. That would suggest that if there is any truth to the claim that folks are staying away because of the church's stance on sinful behaviors, it's more likely because we are too easy on ourselves. In other words, it's more likely because our behaviors simply don't match what we preach. Even more critically, they don't match the behaviors they expect from those who are supposed to look like Jesus. It's easy to turn the finger at those staying away and blame church decline on them, but it might be more profitable to take a good hard look inside the church walls.[1]

There is a song by the late Christian singer and songwriter Rich Mullins entitled *Surely God Is with Us*. Two particular lines from this song that haunt me speak of Jesus:

The whores all seem to love him
And the drunks propose a toast

I doubt if any of us would accuse Jesus of being "soft on sin." Yet, the sick, poor, lame, blind, and beggars and prostitutes all flocked to Jesus. What was it that they saw in Jesus' life and understood from his teachings that drew them in? Somehow the idea that the true reason behind church decline is the church's tendency to speak strongly, consistently, and biblically against sinful behavior just seems unlikely.

In the course of this study, we will examine numerous steps that churches might undertake in order to become more inviting and relevant to the contemporary culture. And by relevant, I do not mean merely accepting of the norms and standards of the culture as our own, but rather the ability to speak faithfully and accurately about the state of the culture in terms the culture can understand. It is oxymoronic to claim that the good news is good news to those who cannot even grasp it.

First Issue: The Church Faces an Uphill Battle

Before getting into the details of the project, however, there are two issues that require our attention—particularly, to those of us who self-identify as followers of Jesus. First, because we live in a culture that tends to over-emphasize the "freedom to do as we please" above all other forms of freedom,[2] we have to admit that the church faces an uphill battle. We have been told our whole lives that individual freedom and autonomy are at the core of what constitutes a human person. As a consequence, the gospel's call to self-sacrifice, "mortification" of the flesh, and elevating the interests of others surely sounds strange and, perhaps more importantly, uncompelling.

Even so, this book does not suggest how better to market your church as a more desirable consumer choice. Am I opposed to marketing church per se? No, of course not. Good marketing creates awareness of the church's ministry—hopefully, with special attention to the ways in which it reaches out and serves those around it. However, I reject the idea that churches are like so many other consumer choices—like the latest "whiter than white" toothpaste, or the restaurant that promises they are committed to letting you "have it your way." If we see the church as just another commodity, marketing the church becomes all about telling folks why "our church" has the best set of benefits for them personally.

Rather, "marketing the church," if we can call it that, must be more along the lines of clearly communicating what the church is, how it relates to questions of ultimate reality, and why God's intentions for human life together include as a centerpiece the religious gatherings we call church. Our answers to the question "What makes church worth getting up for?" will consistently be rooted in the biblically based presupposition that God has created us for participation and fellowship with others in local, communal settings. To go in this direction, though, explicitly recognizes the challenges created by refusing to cater to the idea of church as one more consumer choice and local parishioners as little more than consumers to be wooed and attracted to our "product line." Only as that notion is undermined will it be possible to see the sort of church renewal for which we long.

Second Issue: Our Job Is to Help Solve the Problem

Second, asking the question "What would make church worth getting up for?" implies that I agree that there are many cases where it seems that church is not worth getting up for. *Seems* not worth getting up for? Perhaps we should just be blunt—there are many cases where church certainly *is not* worth getting up for. In fact, we might do well here to heed the words of the Danish philosopher Søren Kierkegaard, who once observed that the practice of Christian faith *could* become so corrupted that rejecting it would be a sign of spiritual discernment. However, the obligations of Christian discipleship do not allow me (or us) to use that as an excuse to avoid regular worship attendance. If we do not find church "worth the time," if we believe the practice of faith has become terribly distorted, then we need to roll up our sleeves and help solve the problem—help make church worth the time it requires. No, finding that church is not worth getting up for does not let us off the hook. Instead, the hook bites more deeply as we are called to find ways once again to create a spirit that "the whores would all love and the drunks would toast."

The Structure

Methodologically, this work is based on a number of interviews that I have had over the last several months with persons in different positions of leadership within the church. Most are pastors of local congregations, though not all are currently in such positions. They are not all from megachurches, and not all from small churches. Each, though, came through personal friendship or by way of recommendation from someone else. While I am heavily indebted to each of them for their contribution, I take responsibility for the conclusions that are drawn along the way and for the syntheses that I suggest among their differing inputs. I have checked with each on those places where I have quoted them directly, but again, in the final analysis, they are not to blame for the final form of this work. I do hope, of course, that they find it consistent with their own thinking on the steps needed to see the church renewed—a common passion we each share deeply, regardless of how we think it best accomplished.

The persons interviewed, and the churches with which they are connected, are as follows (rather arbitrarily listed in alphabetical order, by first name):

Alan Hirsch—author and leader in the missional church movement

Brian McLaren—author and leader in the emergent church movement

Chris Seay—Ekklesia Church, Houston, Texas

Deb Hirsch—lead pastor at The Tribe, Los Angeles, California

Greg Boyd—Lead Pastor, The Woodlands, Minneapolis/St. Paul, Minnesota

Mike Slaughter—Ginghamsburg United Methodist, Tipp City, Ohio

Reverend Nadia Bolz-Weber—Lead Pastor, House for All Sinners and Saints, Denver, Colorado

Olu Brown—lead pastor, Impact Church, Atlanta, Georgia

Rosario Picardo—lead pastor, Embrace Church, Lexington, Kentucky

Tom Tumblin—Dean of the Beeson School, Asbury Theological Seminary, Wilmore, Kentucky

To each of these, I express my heartfelt gratitude for their love of God and God's people as well as for their willingness to take time out of busy schedules to offer words of wisdom and insight to me. May God continue to bless each in their ministries!

I began this project naively hoping that there was a set of common factors that we could put into practice in our local churches that would fuel growth in discipleship.[3] It was not a very realistic hope, though. If things were that simple, many of those who have dedicated themselves to evangelism and church renewal would have long ago discovered that set of factors. Similarly, if it were that simple, I could merely recount to you the common elements derived from my interviews of the folks listed above. That, in turn, could become a formula for creating and sustaining churches worth getting up for. As it turns out, however, what passes for a "church worth getting up for" varies a good deal from one context to the next. Are you located in a highly multicultural setting? Or one more ethnically monolithic? Where do the people in your area fall on the modernist/post-modernist spectrum? What is the demographic of the local community? Do you have a large population of folks who have had bad experiences with church? It should not be surprising that divergent answers to these questions will mean that what works well in one context may not work well in another.

In the following chapters, we will discuss factors that different church leaders have found to be contributors to success *in their particular context*. It is my sincere belief and hope that among the different ideas that these leaders have deployed, there is potential for churches in many different situations. The bottom line? Discernment of the local context, guided by the presence of the Holy Spirit, will be the critical factor in designing a church experience that folks will find worth getting up for. What will make a church worth getting up for in the Midwest may be quite different from what makes one worth getting up for in the Northeast, for example. However, I am confident that church leaders from across the spectrum will find the analysis provided here to be helpful in their attempts to be churches worth getting up for. May God grant us renewal in our day!

Chapter 1

Putting Jesus Back at the Center

When people say: "I would like to have a coke, please," do they really mean they want that brand of soda known as Coca-Cola? Or, by asking for a "coke," are they merely intending to ask for a soda, using the term "coke" as a generic for soda or soft drink? Often, we really don't know without asking. Have you ever thought about how much of a marketing advantage it is for the manufacturers of Coca-Cola to have their brand, "coke," as the generic term used for soft drink or soda? One of the biggest obstacles to the success of a new consumer product is the creation of brand awareness for that product. You can't buy a product you don't know exists—no matter how good it may be. So, all product manufacturers strive to have the brand of their product line become a household word, recognizable by almost everyone. Other brands that have become synonymous with specific product lines include: Xerox (copy company or for copies); Q-tip (cotton swab manufacturer or the swabs on a small stick); Sea-Doo (the company or the generic for jet ski); Jello (the brand or generic for gelatin dessert); and Jacuzzi (the brand or generic for hot tub).[1] There is no guarantee that such brand recognition will result in success. The product still has to be a good one, but such brand recognition creates enormous opportunities for these companies, which is evidenced by the huge sums of money they spend to create and preserve a high level of brand recognition.

Now, before we get too much further into this discussion, let me again assure the reader that my goal is not to identify some clever marketing scheme that will transform churches so that they seem a "superior consumer choice" to the other Sunday morning alternatives. While I strongly resist going in that direction, the challenges we face are brought into sharp relief when we consider the concepts of branding and brand recognition. What sort of "brand experience" do folks have with church—generally speaking? It's really quite a mixed bag, isn't it? If the brand experience of the church is loosely defined as the sum total of all interactions with "the church," then we are going to get answers that fall across the spectrum. However, what studies show us is that the younger demographic (those under thirty-five, for example) are increasingly finding that their brand experience of church is either neutral ("yeah, church is okay, it's just irrelevant") or negative ("I've had enough of church, I quit"). In other words, the church has very high brand recognition (folks know what church is). However, when you look at the long-term health of the church, neutral or, perhaps more commonly, bad brand experiences create significant concern. Because of bad brand experiences, the brand image of the church (again, speaking generically) is perceived quite negatively.

In a later chapter,[2] we will discuss the perceptions that persons have of Christians[3] and our church. Here, however, we will summarize quickly. In a study published by Kinnaman and Lyons,[4] the three most common terms or phrases people used to identify Christians (and by implication, the church) were: hypocritical, judgmental, and antihomosexual. In other words, the "brand image" (brand image is a mental construct made to capture the experiences and expectations associated with a particular brand) of the church in general and Christians in particular leaves rather a lot to be desired. Let's come at this from a somewhat different angle and see what we can learn from it.

Consider the following little experiment (or, better yet, conduct it yourself).[5] Let's imagine that mid-morning in some large U.S. city, we wander out to poll anyone who will stop long enough for us to ask one question. That one question is this:

Of all the people who have ever lived, who would you consider to be the three greatest?

Word the question in that particular way—not who are the *most influential* or not who are the *best known* (since either of these would likely allow folks to include persons who have had negative impacts). Who do you think would be candidates for such a list? Alexander the Great? Socrates or Plato? Copernicus? Newton or Einstein? I'll make the following prediction: in the overwhelming number of cases, Jesus will be listed as one of the top three. In those cases where he is mentioned, he will most often be named as the greatest person ever to live. To use our earlier terms, I am sure we would find not only that Jesus has excellent "brand recognition" but also that he has an overwhelmingly positive "brand image." I wonder what to make of that?

Let's imagine you were able to get a few more minutes with several of the persons who agreed to take our one-question poll. Imagine they were willing to answer one more question:

Why do you think Jesus was one of the greatest people of all time?

What sorts of answers do you suppose you would hear? A vague affirmation of his teachings? We would probably hear that answer with some frequency. Perhaps people would focus on his call to love all those around us, most especially our enemies. Perhaps they would focus on his affirmation of the value of each and every person by the way in which he invited all into relationship with himself. Some would name his utterly unselfish way of living. There would be a variety of answers you would get to this question, but one thing of which you can rest assured is this: the answers would run in precisely the opposite direction from the criticisms of the church mentioned above. In other words, while the Christian church and Jesus would both have very high brand recognition, their brand image would be very, very different. The difference is captured in a quote often attributed to Ghandi:[6] "I love your Christ, I do not like your Christians. Your Christians are so unlike your Christ." And, there you have it in its most succinct form—many love Jesus and their perception of his life and values, but they look at us

Christians and our churches and they see a huge disconnect. What's up with that? Well, the short answer is: to be worth getting up for, we in the church need a major reboot, with the result that the life and behaviors of Jesus return to the center of what following Jesus is all about. Only then can we expect a culture tired of those who play at religion to sit up and pay attention to the good news.

Unfortunately, too often our answer to the different perceptions between Jesus and the Christian church is framed in a self-serving way. For example, I recall one author arguing that there really was no difference between Jesus and his church. Instead, he argued that Ghandi had created a Jesus of his own making, a Jesus that was not particularly biblical. It's no wonder Ghandi preferred that Christ, the argument continued, but we Christians don't need to take this criticism seriously. I suppose the conclusion we are supposed to draw is that Ghandi, and those like him, really should dislike both Jesus and the church. Is it the case that there are those who have created a perception of Jesus that really is just a "tamed down" version of the biblical Jesus? Is it possible that the Jesus so admired by some really is quite disconnected from the real Jesus? Of course, it is possible, perhaps even likely. However, before we dust off our hands, comfortable that we have undermined this particular criticism, we need to think much more deeply. Perhaps there are some other reasons for the fact that folks have such divergent views of the church and its Lord and Founder. And, maybe, just maybe, there is some validity to the fact that people love Jesus, but feel very differently about many who claim to be his followers.

Before moving on, it is worth noting one likely reason that some feel that popular conceptions of Jesus are constructs that are quite different from the biblical Jesus. Those who "love Jesus but hate the church" tend to focus on Jesus' behaviors, the ways in which he engaged those around him: loving them, healing them, feeding them, offering them hope. Those on the other side tend to focus more on doctrine and beliefs. The former see Jesus most fundamentally defined by his interactions and relationships, the things that he did and the ways in which he related to others. The latter see Jesus most fundamentally defined by the theological statements the church developed and affirmed about him.[7] One side can't imagine why it would matter what you believe about Jesus if you are not engaged in a life that looks like his. The other, because of its firm commitment to salvation by faith alone, too easily overlooks the significance of a life that imitates Christ. Both sides have a point, for sure. However, at a time when the disconnect between Jesus and his followers is so great,[8] we need to be much quicker in listening and acting on the criticisms and slower to feel the need to engage in self-justification. So, when critics of the church say that Christians do not look very much like Jesus, what exactly do they mean?[9]

To begin with, Jesus was quite a bit different from the vast majority of Christians today. How so? Jesus saved his harshest criticism for the religious community, and even then, the strongest criticisms were saved for religious leaders. Today, we Christians seem obsessed with the culture at large, identifying its every flaw, blaming it for many of the problems that we face in the church, and we are often unwilling to accept our own contributions to those problems. We assume a "victim" mentality, sure that the culture at large is out to get us. Failing to realize our own shortcomings makes us the perfect target for a portrayal of us as self-righteous and unserious. We select "hot button" moral issues, mostly ones of which we perceive ourselves to be innocent, and we make them central to our critique of the culture around us. That moral agenda often looks thin and self-serving to the culture, and they conclude we Christians are hypocritical and judgmental—often quite rightly so. We would do well to heed Jesus' words to tend to the log in our own eye before worrying about the splinter in the eye of the culture. Or, perhaps we need more to "love the sinner and hate our own sin."[10] Instead, we are perceived as excusing our own sin and hating the sinner, worried more about looking like we have it together than in expressing grace and mercy to those who readily admit they do not.

The Gospel writers remind us repeatedly about the temptations to become judgmental and self-righteous. Jesus points it out in the Sermon on the Mount with the log/splinter reference. In addition, the parable of the Pharisee and the tax collector makes the point with some force. The Pharisee would have been the epitome of all that was religious, and he did not fail to point that out to God in his prayer, recorded in Luke 18. He reminded God of all his good behaviors, even taking time to thank God that he was not like the despised tax collector. On the other hand, the tax collector as the representative of the worst of the worst merely prays for mercy. The outcome? The recitation of good behaviors benefits the Pharisee not a bit, and we are told it is the tax collector who leaves the synagogue accepted by God. In the fourth chapter of his Gospel, Luke has the audacity to place the first demon exorcism right in the middle of the synagogue. N. T. Wright suggests that Luke is trying to convey a central theme in Jesus' ministry: quit worrying about those outside the walls of the gathering place of God's people and focus instead on being faithful to God's call on you.[11] Re-centering on Jesus will mean spending less time critiquing the culture and more time in a self-critique that brings our lives into closer alignment with that of Jesus.

The culture also finds disconnect between Jesus and the church regarding the positions from which we engage in ministry. In short, where did Jesus spend all his time? He was forever among the poor, the lame, those marginalized for one reason or the other. He hung out with the sinners, with the tax collectors (even taking one for a disciple!), with those the religious would have considered outsiders. I remember a friend saying to me once, quite well-intentioned, that he could never hang out at the bars, even if for ministry. He was afraid that folks would assume he was one of "them." Jesus seemed not so worried about that, obviously convinced that his presence among the sinners would do them more good than they could possibly do him harm. So, when the critics of church point out how different we are from our Lord, they notice how we do ministry from a place of comfort.

Some of us wander onto the margins from time to time, visiting briefly the kinds of situations and circumstances in which Jesus made his home. And while I affirm the ministries that engage the margins on a short-term basis, the critics of church notice how little we really have invested there. Chris Seay, pastor of Ecclesia Church in Houston,

Texas, made this point beautifully to me with the following story. It seems he and his family had relocated to a new part of town to begin a new church. The church building was also where he and his family lived. One evening, he went out for a moment and noticed what he described as the tallest group of women he had ever seen. When he got closer, though, he realized they weren't women at all, but rather transvestite prostitutes. Before I could ask anything about it, he said, "Well, what could I do? I invited them in for coffee."[12] To re-center on Jesus, we must become more known for our ministry *from and on* the margins, rather than *to* the margins.

The shortest way to make the overall point is this: if we want to be a church worth getting up for, we will need to close the perceived gap between Jesus and the church. We are going to have to *look a lot more like Jesus* and spend less time talking about *what we believe about Jesus.* Jesus fed the poor and hung out with sinners. His parables tell of restoring the marginalized to communion and fellowship with God's people. He called people to unflinching commitment to God that costs one everything, but he made that call while modeling that sort of commitment himself. Jesus told his followers to love everyone, even their enemies, and loving them did not mean having the warm fuzzies for them. It meant willing their best and participating in making that a reality. None were unreachable to Jesus. Just as God blessed both the evil and the good, so are we to be a blessing to all without regard to merit.

Our Lord has remarkable brand recognition and overwhelmingly positive brand perception. If we church people really want to see renewal, really want to become a part of a church worth getting up for, the answer is near to us. We must re-center around Jesus, particularly his life and behaviors—be not just willing but actually pouring ourselves out for those around us. We must make a space for those we consider to be most unlike us. Even more, we must make a space at the table for those we consider our enemies, creating that space for others, not from a place of comfort, but rather taking up space alongside the very people Jesus did. Do we want to stop the criticisms of the church? Do we want to undermine the claim that Christians are not like Christ?

All we have to do is start to become more like him, but therein lies the rub, doesn't it? To take seriously the call to be imitators of Jesus is a deeply scary thing. Who will protect me, if I take up space on the margins of life? Who will make sure that my family does not suffer if I take on such a potentially dangerous location for ministry?

You know, I really have no answers to those questions. I can say the answer Jesus gave. He said that all who had given up things in this life would receive them back one hundred times in the next.[13] Beyond citing Jesus, I have nothing to offer. At times, I think the question is not whether or not we can create churches worth getting up for. Instead, the real question is: how badly do we want to have churches worth getting up for? Enough to imitate Jesus? Enough to suffer discomfort and social dislocation? Enough to participate with God in the building of churches that turn our normal conceptions upside down? Are there a few intrepid souls willing to wander down this path? If so, if we can convince ourselves to take these radical steps, perhaps God will be gracious and send a few souls our way. Because, remember, at the end of the day, ministry of this sort is every bit as critical to our own salvation as it is to those to whom we minister. Let's do a massive church reboot—one that puts the life of Jesus at the center. Let's take that first step toward becoming a church worth getting up for!

Chapter 2

The Value of Authenticity

Almost without exception, the folks I interviewed for this project named *authenticity* as a critical component of a church worth getting up for. The sense was overwhelming that a major contributor to the ongoing decline of the church was simply weariness with "playing church" and with those who insist on "playing church." Set over against the feeling that we Christians gather together weekly primarily to reinforce each other in keeping up appearances was a call for authenticity, for a faith that is, first and foremost, lived out with honesty and transparency. Of course, that immediately raises the question: What does it mean to be authentic? What does it mean to live with transparency? Most essentially, to live authentically is to live so that *who we are* flows from our own true, inner selves, rather than from external expectations created either by social, cultural, political, or even religious pressures. For us as Christians, a critical part of our true, inner selves connects directly to the realization that we have been created by God, in God's image, and for intimate relationship with him and those around us. In the course of reflection, I have become convinced that this talk of authenticity runs in two different, but closely related, directions.

An Inward Focus

First, and perhaps foremost, we all want a place where we can just be ourselves, a place where we can trust that "being ourselves" is not going to result in judgment or criticism, a safe place to be open about out struggles, doubts, and fears. If we'll be honest, we all live much of our lives behind masks of one type or another. We wear a mask of competency and confidence at our workplace. We cover over whatever dark side we might have, generally in even our most intimate relationships. We go to church behind a facade of having everything under control, our doubts and fears held at bay. But, deep down, I suspect that we all find those masks wearisome. We want to be loved and accepted, but we generally resist exposing our truest selves for fear of rejection. So, we trade authenticity for acceptance, masking who we really are in order to be favorably received, largely allowing sociocultural pressures to define who we are. That doesn't change the fact, though, that we long to be accepted and loved as we really are.[1] This first sense of authenticity, then, is inwardly focused.

An Outward Focus

The second way in which authenticity comes into play for churches is more outwardly focused, and it is at the core of the critique that Christians/church people are hypocritical. We claim to embrace one thing, but do another, the critics say. Quite often, as we noted in the last chapter, this "embracing one thing and doing another" takes the form of claiming Jesus as the model for our lives, but then living in a way that bears little or no resemblance to the life of Jesus. We are, in a nutshell, judged to be inauthentic, fakes, pretenders. For better or worse, the members of contemporary society are increasingly good at ferreting out the pretentious and the absurd. They show up at many of our churches and, within minutes, have figured out the extent to which we are "real" and the extent to which we are "fake." Almost without fail, they more quickly see through our inauthenticity than we do. Soon, they are rolling their eyes at our pretension and wondering why they bothered stopping in, quite sure they won't make that mistake again. But, you know what is interesting? How quickly they tune back in once we admit our pretension. We don't have to be completely healed of our hypocrisy, because they very often realize the inability to be genuine affects them as well. No, we don't have to be entirely *over* our inauthenticity, we just have to have taken the initial step of *admitting* it.

Escape from the Cycle

But, as it turns out, that first step seems agonizingly difficult to take, and that's where the two senses of inauthenticity become intertwined. We are often reluctant to be transparent, feeling more secure behind a self we have created (often unconsciously) to align with sociocultural, or perhaps more to the point here, religious expectations. And, of course, in Christian circles, those expectations are ones that we have created ourselves—the proverbial hoisting by our own petard. However, our pretensions are all too evident to those seeking transparency and authenticity. Consequently, we find ourselves called out for those pretensions, but rather than opening us to authenticity, the criticism reinforces our need to wear a mask. We next modify our mask to give the *appearance* of authenticity, which, of course, only looks all the more pathetic to our critics. It turns into a vicious cycle, the more criticism of our inauthenticity, the more fear of being authentic and, in fact, the more inauthentic we become.

How does one escape the cycle? Through recognizing the different ways in which we are inauthentic, and then by beginning to take those masks down, one at a time. In short, we have to be willing to become vulnerable to those around us, putting ourselves in their hands, at some level. Will we ever be fully authentic? Perhaps, perhaps not, but a church worth getting up for is one that actively seeks to create moments of genuine engagement and authenticity. Let's turn to some of the more obvious ways in which we allow ourselves to live inauthentically.

We pretend that we have it all together. I recall a conversation with a friend who was pastor of a church of a few hundred. A couple, who were mutual friends of the pastor and me, were about to divorce, and I had expressed my sadness to him about it. His response caught me rather a bit by surprise. He said something like, "Oh, yes, it is very sad, but what is even sadder is that there are at least a half dozen other couples in my church at just about the same point." When I asked why he thought this was the case, he responded that the church tended to create an internal culture that holds up successful marriages as the norm for Christians. What this produces, in turn, is an unwillingness to admit marital problems in the early stages. To admit that our marriage is less than ideal, to admit that we are struggling to keep it together, is not just to admit a marital struggle but also to admit a failure as a Christian. As a consequence, the pastor went on to say, we hide the problems in our marriages, putting on a happy face, until the difficulties boil over. At that point, of course, we can no longer hide the problems and often the marriage is beyond repair.

I have used this particular example to make the point, but we could have chosen any one of a number of other examples. Virtually all Christians would readily grant that "spiritual pride" was one of the things that Jesus consistently warned his followers to avoid. No doubt, his warnings were not rooted in some abstract dislike for all things prideful, but instead were based on the damage he knew would be the result.

Despite knowing better, in spite of our recognition of the harm, we still allow pride to hold us back from the very sort of authentic interactions that might enable us to overcome the consequences of our weaknesses and struggles. Do we struggle with alcohol or drug addiction? Best not to admit that, our Christian brothers and sisters might look down on us. Do our lusts threaten to get the best of us? Better to create the image we have our demons under control, especially in this area—Christians tend to be merciless when it comes to sexual struggles. Are we often unable to control anger or rage? We probably just need to pray harder, no need to let others in on the secret. These are the things we tell ourselves to justify continuing the pretense. Churches worth getting up for are those which have figured out how to create safe spaces for the kind of authenticity that allows for confession without condemnation, places that allow being honest without fear of becoming the latest topic of gossip.

We pretend that God is tame and predictable . . . and manipulable. In the Chronicles of Narnia, there is a conversation that goes on between the young Lucy and Mr. Beaver. Mr. Beaver is telling Lucy about Aslan, who she thinks is a human. When Mr. Beaver explains that Aslan is not a man, but rather a lion, Lucy asks fearfully, "Then, he isn't safe?" Mr. Beaver responds, "'Course he isn't safe. But he's good." Aslan the lion is the Christ figure in the Chronicles, and Mr. Beaver's answer to Lucy reminds us of a critical aspect of God's nature—God really isn't tame. Yet, on your average Sunday, at your average church, we not only speak of God as if God were tame, we even go so far as to make God seem downright boring. When you think about it, you have to wonder how we are able to do that—to speak of God as both tame and boring. Even worse, we give the impression that, in the final analysis, we think God is there primarily to serve our wants and needs. It is a very "self-o-centric" view of God, which, quite frankly, our critics simply don't get. They wonder how it is that we can believe we have domesticated the source of every smidge of power in the universe, and, of course, they know we are kidding ourselves.

A church worth getting up for is one that is, if not fully, at least partially aware of *who* is invoked when they speak the word "God." If we really believe the questions around God and God's relationship to humanity are *the* most important questions to address, we had best start acting like it. If church is just a hobby we use to occupy an otherwise boring Sunday morning, then let's be honest about that. And, if it's the latter, let's quit pretending like we care if anyone comes to join us or not. This quotation from Annie Dillard quite accurately gets after the main point:

> On the whole, I do not find Christians, outside of the catacombs, sufficiently sensible of conditions. Does anyone have the foggiest idea what sort of power we so blithely invoke? Or, as I suspect, does no one believe a word of it? The churches are children playing on the floor with their chemistry sets, mixing up a batch of TNT to kill a Sunday morning. It is madness to wear ladies' straw hats and velvet hats to church; we should all be wearing crash helmets. Ushers should issue life preservers and signal flares; they should lash us to

our pews. For the sleeping god may wake someday and take offense, or the waking god may draw us out to where we can never return.[2]

We like life to be tame, under control, safe. If we were to be honest, most of us would like to think God is at our beck and call rather than the other way around. To the outside world (and, frankly, more and more of those inside the church!), we seem to be engaged in false advertising—talking about "Almighty God" in our advertisements, preaching about a domesticated deity when they come out to join us. Can we really blame folks for stepping away?

We pretend that what we believe as Christians is absolutely true and the expression of any doubt is an insult to God. It was a French philosopher named René Descartes who set us on the path toward believing that we should have certainty about the things we believe. During the course of the last few hundred years, Christians have joined in the effort to establish a rational basis for the central tenets of the faith so that any "reasonable" person would accept them as true. While it is more and more accepted that there is no such commonly accepted rational basis from which to argue, we Christians are far often hostile toward the questions raised by nonbelievers and believers alike. When you add the apparent hostility that many Christians express toward the sciences, we create an appearance of living in our own intellectual ghetto with our own truths. While not focusing explicitly on Christians, a relevant study[3] recently found the following. As a general rule, if a person believes something to be true, the production of evidence to the contrary *does not* cause that person to change their belief to match the evidence. In fact, the production of contrary evidence *actually results in the person holding their original position with even more tenacity.*

The reality is that reasonable questions can and are raised about aspects of the Christian faith. There is no reason for us, as Christians, to fear those questions or to pretend that they are somehow an affront to God. In fact, the early church was very selective in the positions that it chose to make a part of official church doctrine. Pretty much without exception, the ones they did make official doctrine were related to how they understood the life and death of Jesus to restore relationship with

God. A church that folks will find worth getting up for will create a culture that not only welcomes but also invites individuals to ask any and all questions they have. When it comes to the doubts and struggles that attend religious faith, authenticity means avoiding the pretension of certainty and accepting the inherent "faith" nature of religious belief.

We pretend that our sins are not that bad, or at least, not as bad as the sins of those whom we condemn. Luther used a Latin phrase to describe Christians—*simul justus et peccator.* It means essentially: at the same time, both saint and sinner. He recognized that God's saving grace embraces us and lifts us to restored relationship with God, but he was also realistic about the ongoing struggle with sin. We church folk come across as disingenuous and inauthentic when we spend so much time in critique of the sins of those around us and so little time in critique of our own sins. Am I a glutton? Well, at least I am not a liar. Am I a liar? Well, at least I do not cheat on business deals. Do I cheat others? Yeah, but I am not driven by greed. Am I greedy? Well, at least I am not an adulterer. And, so the list goes on. The inherent hypocrisy does not go unnoticed by our critics.

The reason for inauthenticity about our own sinful behaviors is easy enough to understand. While we have relatively little problem admitting a nonspecific degree of sinfulness, admitting that specific behaviors are sinful means admitting that they need to be changed. Many of those behaviors we really do not want to change—gluttony, selfishness, greed, inattention to stewardship of the creation, subtle forms of lust and exploitation. It is much easier to focus as a group on a smaller set of "hot button" issues, particularly the ones in which we do not engage. Yet, we have been entrusted with the good news—the announcement of the forgiveness of sins, the offer of restoration to right relationship with God. Being authentic about our own brokenness may seem painful and difficult at first, but it is precisely the sort of honesty that those outside the church need.

We view our own physicality with inauthenticity. I recall a discussion with a friend whose young adult child was participating in a summer ministry program. The child had contacted him, quite upset about some of the things that were being communicated around dating and boyfriend/girlfriend relationships. The details are unimportant for our discussion, but it was clear that this ministry, like many others, was largely unprepared to take on seriously the issues around human sexuality. The father characterized the teaching content the ministry used as willing to create a dozen different kinds of problems for the youth in order to make sure they avoided premarital sex. Unfortunately, we seem to be caught at one or the other of two extremes. On the one side, there is such a strong affirmation of our physical natures that we seem to think any attempt to control our natural urges is inappropriate at best, unhealthy at worst. On the other end, we get such a strong reversal that we seem to judge our physical natures *in and of themselves* to be sinful. Neither end of the spectrum models the authenticity about our physical natures we need to model in our church life together. We need neither become libertines nor puritans, but rather find a middle ground that creates space for openness and dialogue. God's affirmation of the gifts of creation as very good (literally, "good good") needs to be balanced over against the biblical calls to self-denial and self-control.

Again, the critics of church have an excellent nose for sniffing out our insincere or overly simplistic attempts to navigate these difficult waters. The path to authenticity will require more listening and less talking, more carefully finding things to affirm than to critique. And, it will require a sober assessment of all sins as serious without singling out the ones we find particularly problematic or personally disturbing. The path to restored relationship to God runs through Christ, but the particulars of each person's journey must also run directly through the realities of that specific person's life. "One size fits all" solutions are popular for their simplicity, which, sadly, also turns out to be their most significant weakness. Be authentic! Even if it means admitting our own youthful indiscretions.

Conclusion about Authenticity

We live in and participate amongst a generation that is fed up with pretense, hypocrisy, and disingenuousness. Our critics want us to be honest with them—honest about our fears, honest about our uncertainties, honest about the mistakes we have made, and honest about the facts that while sins are serious, forgiveness of sins is the central component of the good news. To create churches that the culture (and increasing numbers of our own members) will find worth getting up for, we will have to focus significant energy on creating spaces of authenticity within the body. Not everyone is ready for full transparency on day one, but everyone longs for relationships where we share ourselves for who we are, not for who we can pretend to be.

How can we take one step at a time? Well, we might consider forming a particular kind of Sunday school class or small group that is intentional about engaging each other with authenticity. That can be done by selecting specific topics to address or by trying to create a spirit of free inquiry, allowing classmates to set the agenda. But, however you do it, get started! We need churches worth getting up for . . . and we need them to have safe places for difficult questions, questions that require and deserve honest, thoughtful, and transparent answers. May God guide us in putting this much-needed ministry of the church in a central role.

Chapter 3

The Big Six

In previous chapters, I have made passing reference to work by David Kinnaman and Gabe Lyons. Their book *unChristian: What a New Generation Really Thinks about Christianity . . . and Why It Matters* is the result of extensive research done at Lyons' behest and by Kinnaman, who now heads the group founded by George Barna.[1] The work provides a nuanced and detailed examination of how Christians (and, thus, generalized churchgoers) are perceived by others, with "others" meaning both those inside and outside the church. Kinnaman gives priority to the demographic most commonly characterized in the literature as "Mosiacs" and "Busters." This is a reasonable place to focus attention, given legitimate concerns about the future of the church.

Anyone familiar with the book knows that the findings are not pretty for us Christians. The book begins with the line, "Christianity has an image problem"[2] and things pretty much go downhill from there, at least as far as an assessment of how Christians are viewed by the next generation. In this chapter, I want to examine the findings of *unChristian* in more detail, looking at the "image problem" the authors detail and then drawing what conclusions we can for our work. It is worth noting that in my interviews, all agreed that the concerns raised by the authors have to be taken seriously by the church. The time for pretending these criticisms are baseless or of minimal concern is well past.

Kinnaman lays out six common perceptions that those interviewed have about Christians, with one chapter dedicated to dealing with each perception. They are, in the order covered in the book:

1. *Hypocritical.* Outsiders consider us hypocritical—saying one thing and doing another—and they are skeptical about our morally superior attitudes.

2. *Too focused on getting converts.* Outsiders wonder if we genuinely care about them. They feel like targets rather than people.

3. *Antihomosexual.* Outsiders say that Christians are bigoted and show disdain for gays and lesbians. They say Christians are fixated on curing homosexuals and on leveraging political solutions against them.

4. *Sheltered.* Christians are thought of as old-fashioned, boring, and out of touch with reality. Outsiders say we do not respond to reality in appropriately complex ways, preferring simplistic solutions and answers.

5. *Too political.* Another common perception of Christians is that we are overly motivated by a political agenda, that we promote and represent politically conservative interests and issues.

6. *Judgmental.* Outsiders think of Christians as quick to judge others. They say we are not honest about our attitudes and perspectives about other people. They doubt we really love people as we say we do.[3]

We really cannot draw too much comfort from the frequent use of the term "outsiders." Kinnaman makes it clear that the perceptions of Mosaics and Busters who are "outside" the church match very closely with those inside the church:

Christianity's image problem is not merely the perception of young outsiders. Those inside the church see it as well—especially Christians in their twenties and thirties. I was unprepared for the research showing that Mosaic and Buster Christians are skeptical of present-day Christianity.[4]

As we get into a discussion of these criticisms and how a church worth getting up for might respond to them, we'll take a look at some common responses, using those as a basis to formulate our own critique and response. For what follows, I have taken a look at several reviews of *unChristian*. I will not quote from any particular one of those reviews, but rather offer my own sense of their general tenor. While many have expressed sympathy for these six criticisms, I am at the moment more concerned with the frequently defensive response we Christians have offered to them. No one likes criticism, me included, but given the state of decline of the church, can we really afford defensiveness?

Hypocritical

At the core of the charge of hypocrisy is the claim that we Christians openly espouse and defend a particular set of moral commitments, but then live quite differently. Perhaps, if we were merely inconsistent, our inconsistency would be more or less overlooked. However, the fact that we are so loud about our moral commitments makes the inconsistency hard to overlook. The first question we have to ask is: Are we really hypocritical? Is this a warranted criticism? The short answer is yes. For a somewhat longer answer, let's consider a summary comment from George Barna about the various surveys that his group has conducted over the years: "Of more than 70 other moral behaviors we study, when we compare Christians to non-Christians we rarely find substantial differences."[5] Let that sink in for a moment—when looking at more than 70 different moral behaviors, we Christians are virtually indistinguishable from non-Christians. Again, when you combine the failure to behave differently from the culture-at-large with the highly critical attitude we have toward others, the charge of hypocrisy is easy to understand.

So, what do we have to say in response to those who say Christians are hypocritical? "Well," one fairly common line of response goes, "Christians don't claim to be perfect, only forgiven." That's certainly true enough, I suppose. Really, though, do we expect our critics to find that response adequate? It may be that, technically, we don't claim to be perfect, but that gets overshadowed by our tendency to be self-righteous, tending to condemn non-Christians for the very same behaviors we either ignore or excuse in ourselves. Perhaps one glaring example of this is how vocal we are with regard to sexual promiscuity and the sanctity of marriage, even though studies have shown self-identified Christians do not behave better in either category. In fact, another of Barna's studies (confirmed by others) showed that more conservative, self-identified Christians actually have a higher divorce rate than other groups.[6]

Sometimes, the claim that Christians are hypocritical is quickly dismissed with a skeptical appeal to cultural bias—are we really more hypocritical than others? Aren't folks just biased against Christians, don't they just want to make us look bad, discredit us? I think there are two things we need to keep in mind before we try to offer this response. First, the culture is not responsible for the fact that self-identified Christians are largely indistinguishable from non-Christians. We can dance all around that well-documented fact, trying to say all kinds of clever things (well, are they really Christians just because they self-identify as such, et cetera, et cetera). However, that is all going to sound self-serving, self-justifying, and hardly winsome. We'd do better to say nothing rather than to offer either of these responses. Second, the culture-at-large doesn't make the claims we do about having unique insight into how God intends us to live. If we are going to make those claims, if we are going to argue that God is working through us to transform the world, then we really owe it to folks to look more like that transformation.

What if we Christians were more humble and honest? What if we just admitted that the personal and social transformation the gospel calls for is an exacting standard that is hard to live up to? What if we openly confessed our failures, as individuals and as the church, admitting that we often fail to live up to the call of the gospel? Instead of engaging in constant critique of those outside the church, we could confess our own sins and recommit ourselves to the work of transformation in our own lives. Of course, that would have to be coupled with genuine transformation, if we are to create churches worth getting up for. Undermining the charge of hypocrisy requires two distinct actions. First, we have to move away from the attitude of self-righteousness that seemingly empowers our aggressive criticism of others. Second, we need to become less hypocritical. In other words, we need to take a good hard look at those 70 behavioral characteristics and begin to make changes so that future studies demonstrate real, concrete differences between Christians and non-Christians.

Too Focused on Getting Converts

The next criticism focuses on the claim that Christians are too "conversionist"; that is, we leave those outside the church feeling as if we engage with them only for the sake of adding "notches" to our belt. Consider this account:

> A young guy approached me in the subway station once, friendly, full of questions, interested in talking. He seemed really nice, and I couldn't believe a New Yorker was being so, well, nice! We exchanged numbers and said we'd hang out sometime. Next time I heard from him, he invited me to a Bible study, and that was all he wanted to talk about. When I said, "No, thanks," I never heard from him again. Rather than being genuinely interested in people for their friendship, we often seem like spiritual headhunters.[7]

The term "evangelism" has a very bad connotation in the minds of many because this is precisely the image that it conjures up. To get a sense of how off-target we can be on this, just consider this: Can you imagine any one of the persons with whom Jesus interacted walking away feeling as if they had been the target of an overly conversionist religious person? I have to admit that in my own youth, there seemed to me little that was more distant from the imitation of Christ than our attitudes toward converting others. Jesus seems never to have felt obligated to conclude his teaching with an "altar call."[8] In fact, when folks indicated they wanted to follow him, rather than extending them the "right hand of fellowship," he often asked them why they wanted to be his followers. It seems we have another case where better imitation of Jesus would undermine criticisms of us Christians.

When asked to name the greatest commandment, Jesus answered with two, or one with two parts, depending on how you interpret the passage: (1) love God with all your being and (2) love your neighbor as yourself. To overcome the impression (reality?) that we are overly interested in converting folks to our way of believing, we have to begin to see persons as centers of worth in their own right, as persons to be loved, unconditionally and completely. If we cannot do that, then we should admit it and not further alienate those outside the church who see immediately through our pretense. Perhaps the way to think of it is along these lines: If you knew that the investment of time you were going to make in some person was never going to lead to their conversion, would you still engage with them? If the answer is no, then I suspect we have not yet grasped the depth of the two greatest commandments. And, if we cannot understand this distinction and model it in our churches, we should not be surprised that many are turned off and find us not worth their time.

Antihomosexual

Of the six perceptions listed by Kinnaman and Lyons, the one most widely held among Mosaics and Busters is the perception that Christians are antihomosexual. We could easily get into a long, tedious debate, attempting to weigh the evidences on both sides regarding the question of whether or not homosexuality is sinful. Let's see, however, if we can make a few observations that will allow us to put that question to the side for our purposes.[9] First, given the changing opinions on the question of same-sex marriage, particularly amongst Christians in this age demographic, it is reasonably clear that same-sex marriage will be legal within the next several years. This means that the bigger question with which Christians must deal is how we are going to do ministry in a context where same-sex marriage is legal. Second, Christians are deeply divided on this issue, with many vocal leaders on each side. This fact does nothing to establish which side is right and which is wrong, but it should belie that notion that the issue is a simple one. Third, and most importantly, let's consider the following, just for the sake of argument. Let us assume that those who argue that homosexuality is a sin are right. Would that justify our behaving in a way that creates the perception that Christians are, to use Kinnaman's words, bigoted and show disdain for gays and lesbians? On what basis would we single out this particular behavior and condemn it above others? You will notice that Kinnaman found no perception that Christians are strongly anti-divorce, nor did he find we were particularly vocal about the sensuality implied by gluttony. I do not recall any religious leaders suggesting that natural disasters were God's punishment for our ready acceptance of divorce, even though it is openly denounced in Scripture. But, even on the assumption that homosexuality is a sin, why should we Christians come across as those who hate homosexual persons?

Because opinions are so divided and felt so deeply, I have to admit it is difficult to know exactly what to say about homosexuality relative to building churches that folks find worth getting up for. For one thing, though, wherever we come down on the issue, we are going to have to overcome the image that has us making gays and lesbians the scapegoats for all that is wrong in our culture. The outward hostility, the tendency to treat gays and lesbians as if they are somehow particularly worthy of disdain has to go. With God's help, we must create safe places where all can come experience God, and then we will need to exercise just a wee bit more trust in the Holy Spirit's leading folks to the right conclusions about their behaviors. Whatever conclusion we draw about whatever sinful behavior, the simple point remains that, as Christians, we should understand that there is no place better for us to be than in church. Jesus has chosen the church as the place where the forgiveness of sins is proclaimed and the Spirit is ever present and ready to lead us to the transformation we need, the transformation God has planned for us all, transformation of all our sinful behaviors—even the ones of our own that we tend to excuse or see as not so serious.

Sheltered

Those outside the church see Christians as isolated and sheltered, often perceived as inappropriately closed to nonreligious sources of information or sources of information outside their tradition. Perhaps the best way to make this point is to tell a story about a professor's comments to his students regarding a particular interpretive theory with which he disagreed, presented as false, and otherwise spent little time examining. He told us that he had received letters from several past students who had expressed concern that his cursory critique of the theory had not prepared them to deal with its strengths. It seems that when they moved to the next level of studies, they had encountered professors more persuaded by the theory. The students said they felt that in his class they had been sheltered from the more forceful aspects of the theory.

We could give numerous examples. With the vast majority of scholars agreeing that evolutionary theory provides a plausible explanation for how God created the world, there is an increasing Christian subculture that seems determined to reject the theory and raise their children sheltered from its forcefulness. Climate change is recognized as a reality by the overwhelming majority of experts, but again, many see politically conservative Christians as unwilling to be persuaded by the evidence. As Kinnaman notes, Christians are viewed as insisting on simplistic solutions to complex problems—simplistic solutions that turn out not to be solutions at all.

In order to undermine this perception, we Christians will need to become more open to moving and being outside of a bubble of our own creation. We certainly don't have to embrace every new theory or idea that comes down the pike, but an unwillingness even to consider any data outside our own sanctioned sources will result in little more than a rolling of the eyes by our critics. Today, Christians are largely viewed as sectarian and withdrawn from the "real world." Yet, in past centuries, Christians were at the forefront of many fields of inquiry, often engaging in the sciences and politics, and not just in the area of religious faith. Somewhere toward the latter part of the Enlightenment, Christians seemed to become increasingly concerned that the sciences and religious faith were opposed, rather than complementary. The rise of modern atheism has often reinforced this perception, but it need not be so. Let's begin by stepping outside our bubbles more often, let's offer a genuinely open mind to ideas that make us uncomfortable, and let's engage the world with real curiosity and delight.

Too Political

With my friend Mike Slaughter, I have written in some detail about the extent to which Christians have allowed partisanship in the culture to infiltrate the church.[10] My view is that if we dig deeper, the claim that we are "too political" boils down more to an issue of being too partisan. Many political issues are complicated, and what precisely constitutes a "Christian position" is the subject of much disagreement. In fact, if you look at party affiliation, there are self-identified Christians in virtually all political parties, and overall, Christians are pretty evenly divided between the two major parties. So, the idea that Christians can vote only one way or can support only one party's candidates is simply mistaken. And, the idea that Christians should not participate in the political process seems clearly mistaken.[11] However, by allowing ourselves to become partisan (in either direction), we increasingly appear to those outside the church to be driven, not by the love of Christ, but rather by a partisan political agenda. In turn, we start to sound like we are defining the "real Christians" as those who agree with our political positions. To give up partisanship is to admit Christians really can and do come to different political conclusions and to realize that the unity we share as followers of Jesus ought always to trump our political preferences. Again, there is nothing wrong with participation in the political process or with holding political positions passionately. The problem arises when we allow our political commitments to divide us from Christians who come to different political positions. A bit more humility about our political positions and a bit more acceptance of those who disagree with us will go a long way toward undermining the perception that Christians are too political.

Judgmental

The final of the "big six" is the perception that Christians are judgmental. I am not sure we need to expand a great deal on discussions to this point, since the claim that we are judgmental is closely related to several of the other five. The major point goes back to how "loud" we are about our own judgments about what constitutes the moral life and how easily we condemn those who live in opposition to those judgments. According to our critics, we are quick to judge, often judge quite harshly, and do not adequately allow for the complex circumstances involved in much moral decision-making. We appear to be overly simplistic in our judgments and frequently devoid of the love we claim to feel toward those whom we judge. Those outside the church doubt our concern for them, feeling instead that we enjoy the sense of moral superiority that comes from condemning others.

I recall reading one defense against the charge that we are judgmental that went something like this: of course we will seem judgmental to the culture; we take firm positions on sin and seeming judgmental is a consequence. The person went on to argue that Jesus judged sin and that he and his followers were killed for it. I find this view flawed at a number of levels. In the first place, going back to our discussion on hypocrisy, the degree to which we seem judgmental is, I believe, firmly connected to our eagerness to denounce the sins of others from a position of smug self-righteousness. If we were anywhere near as eager to admit our own fallenness, our own complicity in wrongdoing, I suspect we would find those outside the church less critical. Second, I rather doubt Jesus and his followers were killed for taking firm positions on sin in the sense intended by those criticizing us as being judgmental. Sinners flocked to Jesus and often to his followers. They did not avoid him because of his tendency to be judgmental; rather they came to him as one who was a friend to sinners. You see, most of us know we are sinners; we just tend to get defensive about it when it's pointed out. However, when Jesus appeared, proclaiming the good news that God is ready to forgive sins, sinners found that worth coming to hear. Third, we would do well to remember that those who killed Jesus were not the rank-and-file sinners of the day, mad that Jesus had the audacity to point out their sins. No, he was killed by religious leaders mad that Jesus had the audacity to point out that they were too engaged in precisely the kind of self-righteous indignation that God hated. In fact, we would do well to remember that those who killed Jesus did so thinking they were doing God a favor—stamping out a form of heresy.

Christians look too much like the Pharisees of the first century and, unsurprisingly, garner much the same response.

When we look at these six criticisms of church as it is commonly practiced in the United States today, they all would benefit from the same solution. To borrow a phrase from Alan Hirsch, we need to "re-Jesus" our churches, that is, we need to once again make Jesus the center point of church. We do a reasonably good job of that when it comes to the things we believe about Jesus but not nearly as good when it comes to imitating the life of Jesus. Consider each of these six criticisms. Jesus lived his life in faithful accord with the things he taught. Even those who question some of our beliefs about Jesus would not see him as hypocritical. Next, Jesus never seemed driven by the need to win converts. He made people feel genuinely loved, evidenced by the crowds who followed him everywhere. Was Jesus perceived as anti-homosexual? Well, we certainly have no evidence that he ever addressed the issue directly, but seemed to have all manner of sinners hanging out with him, even despised tax collectors. He seemed unconcerned that their sinfulness might infect him and totally convinced instead that those who hung around with him would be infected by his holiness. Sheltered? I would think he would be perceived as rather the opposite, always out amongst the people of the land, facing their challenges with them. And while many have pointed out the profoundly political consequences of what Jesus taught, none would have perceived him as a partisan or someone inclined to invest a lot of time in the political process. Finally, while I doubt anyone would accuse Jesus of condoning sinful behaviors, there is no evidence he was perceived to be judgmental in anything like the sense Christians are today. Overall, it's hard to imagine a more potent antidote to these criticisms than a good dose of "re-Jesusing."

At this point, I can hear some saying, "Man, you sure are hard on church folks. Why so rough on them and not so much on those outside the church?" Well, maybe. Perhaps it is the case that I am harder on the sinners inside the church than the ones outside. Perhaps. Really, though, the criticisms in this chapter pretty much all boil down to one thing—we, as church folk, have a hard time admitting how little we are different from those outside the church, and how little difference being "in the church" seems to matter in the overwhelming majority of our lives. Rather than admit that our stumbling, bumbling attempts to follow Jesus are just that, we try to come off as having it all figured out. Rather than owning that we are still in the beginning stages of transformation into what God has called us to be, we are just like the religious ones of Jesus' day in coveting the positions and reputations of honor. That really didn't work out so well for them, and it doesn't seem to be working out all that well for us either.

As I said at the start, the overwhelming majority of those whom I interviewed agreed that the critiques detailed in *unChristian* were far more accurate than we Christians would like to admit. Similarly, there was agreement that these criticisms have to be taken on directly if we are to be perceived as worth the time of those outside the church. Dealing with them, however, cannot be by figuring out increasingly clever arguments for why we can ignore the findings as false. Instead, it will have to come through owning just how often those critiques are right on the money, coupled with a concrete demonstration that we can and will be different. Really, what do we have to lose?

Chapter 4
Radical Hospitality

"When I went to church, no one looked like me and my friends did. We had to culturally commute to the church."[1] This was an observation made by Nadia Bolz-Weber as we discussed her experiences with church during an earlier part of her life. It is an interesting observation, isn't it—"we had to culturally commute to the church."

Have you ever thought about how much our different churches end up looking like social clubs that are focusing attention and outreach on one particular sociocultural group? Oh, for sure, there are some remarkable exceptions, churches that look more like the diversity envisioned in Scripture, where we are told that those gathered around God's throne are composed of every kindred, tribe, nation, and language group.[2] As I say, there are churches that are exceptions, though they are nowhere near as plentiful as we should expect, given how Scripture enjoins us to be welcoming to all.

It has certainly been said that the Sunday morning worship hour is one of the most segregated hours in America, not just racially, but in many other ways as well. We also tend to congregate along socioeconomic lines as well as partisan political lines as well as cultural and ethnic lines. In short, we generally congregate with those who are like us, which is why Bolz-Weber could make the comment that she and her friends had to make a "cultural commute" to church. They were not like the "normal members" of the churches she attended. So, in order to fit, she and her friends had to change, had to conform to the expectations and norms required by those churches, had to become—or at least appear to become—members of the church's dominant culture. Most folks give up; thankfully, she didn't.

Let's dig a little deeper into this idea of radical hospitality. Perhaps the first thing one wonders is why the term "radical" has been stuck in front of "hospitality." To be completely honest, I think the primary reason is to capture everyone's attention. How many of us actually see ourselves as inhospitable? We are all hospitable, right? We are welcoming to those who seek out and find our churches, right?[3] Our own affirmations of our hospitality notwithstanding, the worship hour remains the most segregated of all, and folks with testimonies like Bolz-Weber's are hardly rare. Perhaps even more common are those who, after experiences of "not fitting," simply give up on church as "not for them." Those who add the word "radical" to "hospitality" first and foremost are trying to focus our attention on the simple fact that, whether or not we see ourselves as hospitable, far too often we don't come across that way. Multicultural diversity, rather than an open goal for many of our churches, continues to be resisted in favor of more culturally monolithic congregations. So, however radical our hospitality has been so far, it seems overwhelmingly to result in congregations whose members are too much alike, and our hospitality can be seen as not yet radical enough.

Consider this story related to me by a friend and colleague. In one of our well-to-do churches, one of the administrative committees was holding a meeting in their parlor. The church was an urban congregation, and the room was spotless, well appointed, and professionally decorated. During the course of the meeting, a homeless woman came in from the streets. She immediately caught everyone's attention as not one of the church's regular members. Her clothes were dirty and she had not bathed recently. Much to the chagrin of the committee members, she soon made herself comfortable by sitting on one of their lovely chairs. However, she was not rude, and she bided her time saying nothing until one committee member finally asked her if he could help her. She quickly nodded her head and went on to raise her question. While she indicated that she was doing quite well, she said that she had many friends on the street who were not. She said that what they needed were friends and a place to congregate from time to time, and she wondered whether this church might be one that could help. Would they welcome her friends, offer them a kind word and some encouragement? The committee members went silent, staring at each other in an uncomfortable quiet that was palpable. The question had likely come up before, because it did not take too long for the answer to come. There was, it seems, another church, on down the street a bit farther. That church was one in which her friends might be . . . more comfortable. She stood to her feet, stoop-shouldered, thanked them for their time, and left. Radical hospitality? No, not even barely hospitable.

Father Daniel Homan and Lonni Collins Pratt give us an introduction to the concept of hospitality:

> When we speak of hospitality we are always addressing issues of inclusion and exclusion. Each of us makes choices about who will and who will not be included in our lives. . . . Hospitality has an inescapable moral dimension to it. . . . All of our talk about hospitable openness doesn't mean anything as long as some people continue to be tossed aside. . . . But calling hospitality a moral issue does not tell us the whole truth about hospitality either. A moral issue can become bogged down in legalisms, and hospitality is no legalistic ethical issue. It is instead a spiritual practice, a way of becoming more human, a way of understanding yourself. Hospitality is both the answer to modern alienation and injustice and a path to a deeper spirituality.[4]

As the writers note, at the very core of hospitality are questions around whom we will welcome and include in our communities and whom we will exclude. As Miroslav Volf says in *Exclusion and Embrace*, the matter revolves around access to resources, whether those resources are material, spiritual, emotional, or other. Whom will we draw into community with us? With whom will we share our lives, offering support, nurture, fellowship? The temptation is always to be driven by fear, to see those as "other" to us as presenting threats to "our" way of life.

But, as long as there are those who "continue to be tossed aside," our talk of hospitality will have the same hollowness as James observes in his epistle:

> Imagine a brother or sister who is naked and never has enough food to eat. What if one of you said, "Go in peace! Stay warm! Have a nice meal!"? What good is it if you don't actually give them what their body needs? In the same way, faith is dead when it doesn't result in faithful activity.[5]

Of what value is our hospitality if it continually leaves persons outside the community, excluded from our embrace, avoided because of their "otherness"? Homan and Pratt do us a favor when they remind us that while hospitality is a moral concept, seeing it as merely a moral precept to be observed is to flatten a much richer notion. Hospitality is not just a moral obligation but also a spiritual practice, a means of grace, a channel by which God's grace flows through us, transforming us, and then transforming our world as well. Hospitality is both an ointment for our social structures and a balm for our own souls as well.

The dichotomy of exclusion and embrace takes many different forms. In our earlier example, the basis for exclusion was socioeconomic. Consider, though, the racial exclusion recounted from his early church-life experiences by Philip Yancey. He writes about how the elders of his church responded to the civil rights movement and the demonstrators who might appear at their church in an attempt to integrate with white Christians. The wording of the handouts prepared by the board of deacons reads as follows:

> Believing the motives of your group to be ulterior and foreign to the teaching of God's word, we *cannot extend a welcome to you* and respectfully request you to leave the premises quietly. Scripture does NOT teach "the brotherhood of man and the fatherhood of God." He is the Creator of all, but only the Father of those who have been regenerated.

> If any of you is here with a sincere desire to know Jesus Christ as Savior and Lord, we shall be glad to deal individually with you from the Word of God.[6]

Space does not permit a critique of all the problematic aspects of this statement (not the least of which is the implicit presupposition that any black persons who might show up are not Christian). However, it is an interesting and profound contradiction, isn't it? On the one hand, the exclusion of African-Americans from this Christian community is explicit and clear. On the other hand, true to form for this brand of fundamentalism, there is the strange combination of evangelism with exclusion. In essence, saying to all black brothers and sisters, "Please go away, but if you are lost, go away with Jesus, okay?" I think we could hardly characterize this as a winsome evangelistic appeal, and we could not blame anyone for wondering why they would want to follow a Jesus whose followers so explicitly excluded them from community. It is not without some justification that we believe we have made steps in racial reconciliation, but the degree of segregation in our churches makes clear we have a long way to go to be able to say we have embraced a "radical hospitality."

That we as Christians are to embrace a radical hospitality is very clear from Scripture. In Deuteronomy 10, God instructs the Israelites, as they are about to come into the land, to welcome the foreigner who comes to live or sojourn among them. God bases this on reminding them what it was like to be a stranger in the land of Egypt—and not to be welcomed, but to be exploited. In the parable of the great judgment in Matthew 25, one of the bases for judging between the sheep and the goats is the fact that when Jesus came as a stranger, the sheep welcomed him. Of course, he reminds them that when he says, "I was a stranger," he means "one of the least of these." Those most on the margins, for whatever reason, are the very ones Jesus commends his followers for making feel at home. We get two different images from which to learn about radical hospitality. In the first, Jesus tells a Pharisee who has invited him to dinner what a banquet that pleases God looks like:

> Then Jesus said to the person who had invited him, "When you host a lunch or dinner, don't invite your friends, your brothers and sisters, your relatives, or rich neighbors. If you do, they will invite you in return and that will be your reward. Instead, when you give a

banquet, invite the poor, crippled, lame, and blind. And you will be blessed because they can't repay you. Instead, you will be repaid when the just are resurrected.[7]

What more intimate setting than a gathering for a meal? Throughout many different traditions, not the least of which was the Middle Eastern world of the New Testament, the invitation to share a meal with someone was THE sign of being welcomed into one's life and world. The sort of hospitality God expects, Jesus says, is the kind that welcomes those who cannot repay, the kind that invites those whom the Pharisee would have considered excluded, outside their world. From there, Jesus goes directly to the parable of a person who threw a great banquet—a parable told as a metaphor for the great banquet of the kingdom of God. When those who were originally invited beg off, offering one excuse or another for not attending, the one throwing the party tells his servants to go out to the streets and invite any and all who will come—the lame, the crippled, and the blind. There is no basis for exclusion, other than self-exclusion. By our standards, this is radical hospitality indeed!

According to the story behind the popular song "Where the Streets Have No Name" by rock band U2 is the reality of life in the songwriter's home country. If you know their street address, you know all you need to know about people to judge whether or not they are "your" kind of people. For example, are they rich or poor? Are they Protestant or Catholic? What ethnic background do they embody? The song envisions a place where the streets have no names, where personal details about others are not a consideration when welcoming them into relationships. It envisions a place where the walls have been torn down, and poor, rich, black, white, Protestant, Catholic, sinner, and saint are all welcomed to sit side by side. That place that most preeminently models the "where the streets have no names" way of being together *should be* our churches. We have more than adequate theological and biblical mandates to become the model of radical hospitality. The only real question is how badly we want to be that oasis of peace and reconciliation.

So far, we have focused attention primarily on a couple of areas to which the idea of radical hospitality should connect—socioeconomic and racial. These, however, are hardly the only ways in which we pick and choose those whom we wish to include in our communities and those whom we wish to exclude. In our book, *Hijacked: Responding to the Partisan Church Divide*, Mike Slaughter, Robbie Jones, and I explore the extent to which partisanship in our culture has increasingly infiltrated our churches. To connect the point to the issue of hospitality, consider the following example. Imagine you are a member of a church whose members would generally think of themselves as politically progressive. Then imagine a visitor who drives into your church parking lot in a Hummer plastered with a combination of bumper stickers that say things like "Drill, baby, drill!" or "Conservative, Christian, American." What are the first things that will run through your mind? Assuming you are that member of that progressive church, how welcoming do you suppose you and your churchmates will be? Or, let's flip the scenario. Imagine you are a member of a church whose members are largely self-identified as politically conservative. Then, imagine a visitor who drives into your parking lot driving a Prius plastered with a combination of bumper stickers that say things like, "This car gets 50 mpg. So, who's the patriot?" or "Jesus was a liberal." What are the first things that would run through your mind? How welcoming would you and your conservative churchmates be? On more than one occasion, I have heard folks who are already members of particular churches express dismay at how badly they are treated by other church members who do not agree with them politically. If we cannot be civil to those already members with us of a given church, what sorts of welcoming messages do you think we communicate to new visitors? In the latter part of Matthew 5, during the Sermon on the Mount, Jesus observes that in only welcoming those like ourselves, we do no better than pagans. Clearly, his expectations for our ability to welcome and make feel at home those who come to us extend well beyond those with whom we feel a kindred spirit because of common beliefs, cultures, economic status, and so forth.

Having touched on these different ways in which Christian churches ought better to embody a radical kind of hospitality, there is yet another group that we far too easily exclude. What could be worse than our divisions along socioeconomic or racial lines, you ask? Divisions along the lines of things we consider to be sins.[8] Too often, as we noted in an earlier chapter, we Christians are noted for our aggressive attitude of condemnation toward those around us whom we judge to be sinners. But, doesn't the call to radical hospitality extend beyond welcoming those we think already have their lives together? Is it really acceptable, from a biblical standpoint, to exclude from community those we see as sinners?

To some extent, we all have to admit to being sinners. And, further, to the extent we are not sinners *now*, we have to confess to being sinners reconciled to God through God's own initiative, not through any particularly praiseworthy behaviors on our own. Perhaps when the reality of that fully sinks in, we can with much greater abandon welcome those who are still trapped and in bondage to their own fears, greed, selfishness, and lust. I am not suggesting, of course, that those with a record of pedophilia be welcomed in as caregivers to our children or that we take other reckless steps that might endanger one's immediate safety. In the final analysis, though, the question we have to ask ourselves is twofold. First, to what degree are we genuinely interested in spreading the good news? And, yes, in saying "genuinely interested in spreading," I mean beyond the comfortable confines of our own affinity groups. I hope the answer is that we are genuinely interested in spreading the gospel. If we are, then, the practice of radical hospitality to all is a must. Second, let's assume your judgments about what is and what is not sinful behavior are correct. What better place for sinners on a given Sunday than in the bosom of the church, welcomed by God's people, who were rightly characterized by Luther as both sinners and saints at the same time? What better place than where the Holy Spirit, the only real hope of transformation for any of us, is invoked and where, if allowed, the Holy Spirit can act like a plague of holiness, infecting us in the midst of our sinful condition with transformative power?

How can you put into practice radical hospitality in your local church? How can you begin to get folks to see beyond the common

Christian stereotype as judgmental and hypocritical? Begin by identifying the walls that have been created that prevent inclusion and empower exclusion, and then become very intentional about tearing those down, one at a time. Make it an explicit goal of your congregation to make all who show up at your doors feel welcomed and embraced. Worry less about how things look to others and more about how things look to the God who instructed us to love all—even those who are the enemy to us.

And, in the final analysis, ask: How can we really say we have loved someone whom we choose to exclude from our communities?

Chapter 5

Rebalancing

What are the different roles and responsibilities that need to be filled in a thriving and healthy church? When we reflect on that question, it seems we often think in terms of how we structure our weekly worship services. We need a preacher to proclaim the Word; we need a music director and musicians; we need individuals to welcome and greet those who come to our churches, and so on. Of course, this is a valid way to look at the question—we do need persons in these different roles (more or less depending on your worship format) in order to live out our regular gathering together for praise and worship.

Part of our health and vitality (and a critical part, at that) *is related* to the excellence with which we carry out our regular services of praise and worship. Yet, isn't there more to growing a healthy church than making sure we have someone to preach, someone to lead singing, someone to teach? Don't we need not just those who are thinking about the next worship service, but also those who are charged with thinking about the future of the church—locally and globally? Folks whose main task is to "see the big picture," to "envision the next form our worship should take," and, in short, to "dream dreams." In other words, might it be the case that the long-term growth of the church is intimately connected to factors other than good execution of the weekly services of worship and praise? I think the answer to this question is a resounding "Yes!" Let's take a few minutes to explore why.[1]

The Fivefold Ministry

In discussions with Alan and Deb Hirsch about the decline of the church in the West, they both drew my attention to the so-called "five-fold" ministry that has often been identified from Ephesians. The five ministry roles outlined in this passage are: apostle, prophet, evangelist, shepherd, and teacher:

> He gave some apostles, some prophets, some evangelists, and some pastors and teachers. His purpose was to equip God's people for the work of serving and building up the body of Christ until we all reach the unity of faith and knowledge of God's Son. God's goal is for us to become mature adults—to be fully grown, measured by the standard of the fullness of Christ.[2]

Now, right off the bat, we see a couple of the roles mentioned in our discussion about the roles needed for our weekly worship services: pastor (equating "pastor" with "shepherd") and teacher. You might even include evangelist in the role of pastor, depending on the nature of the regular worship services and how often they are supplemented by more evangelistic services.

However, Hirsch explicitly includes evangelists in the list of "over-looked leadership roles."[3] Given the low number of professions of faith reported by many churches over the course of a year, one can understand why he would include evangelist in this list. In addition, it is worth asking how many churches are missing the growth/expansion leadership roles altogether. Hirsch thinks they are too often absent. Here's how he said it in that article:

> We needed missionaries to the West, but our seminaries were not producing them. If we take the five categories of church leadership from Ephesians 4:11, they were training leaders to be teachers and pastors for established congregations, but where were the evangelists, the prophets, and the apostles to lead the mission of the gospel into the world?[4]

In Hirsch's view, we were heavy on "maintenance" but much too light on growth and expansion. If the reader wants more of his assessment on how and why this happened, I commend them to the referenced article.

Most frequently in our churches today (unless they are quite size-able) we tend to combine the role of shepherd and pastor, and some-times evangelist, in the overarching role of "lead pastor." But, the list Paul names here extends beyond these to make the role of evangelist explicit and to include two other roles—the apostle and the prophet. In a concise statement, we have here five different roles identified, along with a clear statement of purpose. Why have these gifts been given to the church? In order to equip the followers of Christ so that all might reach their full potential and be all that God has created them to be.[5] So, that's the why of the so-called fivefold ministry. The question we need to consider next is how these five roles fit together to create a matrix for establishing and growing healthy, vibrant congregations. And, if each is required for vibrant churches, then how are we doing at balancing the presence of each in the contemporary church?

On his website, Hirsch expands each of the roles, giving his take on the implications for ministry of each of the five different, but deeply interrelated, giftings of the Holy Spirit to the church:

> Apostles extend the gospel. As the "sent ones," they ensure that the faith is transmitted from one context to another and from one gen-eration to the next. They are always thinking about the future, bridg-ing barriers, establishing the church in new contexts, developing leaders, networking trans-locally. Yes, if you focus solely on initiating new ideas and rapid expansion, you can leave people and organiza-tions wounded. The shepherding and teaching functions are needed to ensure people are cared for rather than simply used.
>
> Prophets know God's will. They are particularly attuned to God and his truth for today. They bring correction and challenge the domi-nant assumptions we inherit from the culture. They insist that the community obey what God has commanded. They question the sta-tus quo. Without the other types of leaders in place, prophets can become belligerent activists or, paradoxically, disengage from the imperfection of reality and become other-worldly.
>
> Evangelists recruit. These infectious communicators of the gospel message recruit others to the cause. They call for a personal response to God's redemption in Christ, and also draw believers to engage the

wider mission, growing the church. Evangelists can be so focused on reaching those outside the church that maturing and strengthening those inside is neglected.

Shepherds nurture and protect. Caregivers of the community, they focus on the protection and spiritual maturity of God's flock, cultivating a loving and spiritually mature network of relationships, making and developing disciples. Shepherds can value stability to the detriment of the mission. They may also foster an unhealthy dependence between the church and themselves.

Teachers understand and explain. Communicators of God's truth and wisdom, they help others remain biblically grounded to better discern God's will, guiding others toward wisdom, helping the community remain faithful to Christ's word, and constructing a transferable doctrine. Without the input of the other functions, teachers can fall into dogmatism or dry intellectualism. They may fail to see the personal or missional aspects of the church's ministry.[6]

We can rather straightforwardly see the interconnections among the different roles, but we need to discuss in more detail how these functions are needed in healthy, functioning churches.

Now, before proceeding much further, it is important to recognize that not all scholars would agree with Hirsch's way of dividing up these roles.[7] Some would argue it gives too much weight to one New Testament passage, making Paul's comments too much the focus when other texts have to be brought to bear as well. Others would raise yet other objections. However, I don't think we need to detain ourselves pondering the various criticisms. Rather, let's take the ideas that Hirsch puts before us and see if we can use them as a more generalized way to get at some of the problems the contemporary church faces.

Maintenance and Growth/Expansion Roles

In particular, I'd like to focus on how Hirsch divides these five roles up into two more overarching categories. He characterizes one category, which includes the last two of the ministry roles (shepherd and teacher), as "maintenance" oriented. Shepherds are needed to tend to the daily pastoral needs of the members of a given congregation, or as Hirsch says, they nurture, protect, and give care to those under their watch. Teachers are needed to deepen understanding of the Christian faith. They provide education, lay and otherwise, that helps Christians become clearer on the doctrines that support and explain the faith and on the Christian practices that deepen the life of discipleship, and they educate us about how Christian faith has been lived out over the history of the Christian movement. In other words, they help to create an environment that maintains and deepens the faith of those in the church.

The second category includes the other three (apostles, prophets, and evangelists). These are the roles related more to growth and expansion. Apostles envision the future and drive the church forward, helping it to develop the tools needed to bridge the gap to the next generation. Evangelists are the recruiters within the movement. They present the good news of the gospel message and invite others to join up, to exercise faith for themselves and take a place alongside those who identify as followers of Jesus. Prophets are the ones who speak the difficult and challenging truths that we all need to hear from time to time to make sure we stay on track. They remind us that our first (and really, only) allegiance is to Christ, and they most remind us of that when something has gone astray. They are the church's much-needed voice of critical self-reflection. Of course, sometimes the prophetic voice can come to us from beyond the walls of the church, but recognizing that does not reduce the need for the prophetic voice within the church as well. For a church to be healthy, the functions of both maintenance and expansion must both be present and must be present in the right degrees. I will use Hirsch's designations as we begin to explore in more detail, but again, I invite the reader to consider the highest-level claims being made about the role these different leadership vocations have in the creating and sustaining of churches worth getting up for.

Let us begin by reflecting on the importance of the two highest-level categories; that is, let us begin by talking about how we need both "maintenance" and "growth/expansion" roles in the life of the church. From there, we will use Hirsch's model as a way to dig deeper, even while resisting the idea that the "fivefold ministry" is the *only* way to examine these issues. First, rather than thinking of "maintenance" and "growth" as polar opposites, perhaps it is better to think of them as complementary functions that have to occur within the church in order to maintain proper balance. Who could possibly deny that our congregations are now and have always been deeply in need of pastoral care? Conflicts within the church, conflicts between us as church members, challenges that arise in our own personal lives, loss and tragedy in our families—all of these things create emotional and spiritual tensions. Those tensions are often overwhelming and, if we are to navigate them successfully, require love and care from those charged with watching over us. We need encouragement to resist, as Chris Wright puts it, the many and subtle idolatries that threaten to subvert our faith in Christ and his church.[8] We negotiate and celebrate the various "rites of passage" through which we all must go. There are moments to celebrate new births, physical and spiritual; moments to celebrate transitions, such as marriage; and moments to celebrate our life together in community. Similarly, there are moments of mourning, like the death of a loved one, the miscarriage of a potential new life, and the many other tragedies that intrude upon our lives. And, of course, there are bittersweet moments that combine both celebration and mourning. In short, the life of the church is replete with moments where the maintaining presence of a pastoral caregiver is critical to the life of the church.

Whatever we end up calling it, in addition to the leadership role the pastoral caregiver brings to the local congregation, training in discipleship is a critical part of maintaining folks in the life of faith. What do we believe? Why do we believe the particular things we do? How does one navigate moving from knowledge to practice? What are the common Christian practices and how do those empower us with God's grace for the life of faith? The early church saw a critical place for catechetical training.[9] In fact, in the earliest period, a prolonged period of training prior to baptism and admittance to the Communion table was frequently required of new converts. To maintain persons in their faith after initial conversion requires intentionality around training, and perhaps even apprenticing in the life of faith. So, the leadership roles that embody training in the life of faith and pastoral caregiving are critical to keeping churches going. But, what if all of our attention goes to maintenance and only minimal to growth/expansion?

My favorite science fiction series is the Dune series by Frank Herbert. In the series, Herbert explores the idea of messianic leadership roles and how they influence the movements they begin. The main character in the initial book is Paul Atreides, who is Herbert's initial messiah figure. The character, after taking the mantle of leadership, becomes known as Maud'Dib and acquires the gift of "oracular vision," the ability to see into the future. However, the nature of his foresight or prescience is not exact and precise. Rather, what he sees are potential time lines that flow together in such a way that he can judge their relative certainty. Time lines, or possible futures, near the center of his prescient vision are very likely, while those on the periphery are much less certain. In addition, those farther away from the center, the ones less certain, also entail more risk. In other words, he can use his ability to see into the future in ways that allow him to make choices to lead to the central, safer time lines and their corresponding futures. To do so is to allow a great deal of confidence that things will turn out as he foresees them. To make choices that lead to the time lines on the margins means to take the risk that things could turn out very differently than he foresees. It seems a "no brainer" then, right? Just pick the central, more certain time lines and always know what to expect. But, Maud'Dib recognizes an important principle that I find helpful to our conversation here. While one could always make the choices that would lead to the most likely, and thus most safe, time line, to do so is to assure oneself of mediocre outcomes. Mediocre outcomes, consistently chosen, while safe, would eventually lead to stagnation and death. So, Maud'Dib's secret to using his oracular vision is to exercise wisdom about when to play it safe and when to take a risk. Only by taking the occasional, wise risk can one make possible a future that leads to flourishing.

Notice, sometimes taking risks *makes possible* a future of flourishing; it does not assure it.

I fear that too often we allow ourselves to be driven by fear, and the result is that our churches make choices that appear "safe." Sometimes we do this because of fear of the unknown, sometimes it's the fear of failure, sometimes it's just a more intuitive sense of concern. Yet, I wonder if we in the church cannot learn from Maud'Dib's insight. To always pick the safe path might protect us from our fears, might create a sense of security, but will it, in the end, lead to stagnation and death? How many times have we seen grand visions (or, perhaps, not so grand, but still different from "how we've always done things") shot down for fear of failure? What I think Hirsch is trying to get us to see is that when the maintenance leadership roles are over-emphasized, the risk taking inherent in the expansion/growth roles is shunted to the side. The result? We suffer the stagnation and death of mediocrity. Our churches move forward, more or less on inertia, but the charismatic energy is lost, the entrepreneurial spirit is quenched, and that forward movement, over time, increasingly slows. Perhaps, at last, it comes to a halt and actually begins to decline, losing ground once gained as a consequence of our playing it safe.

An important part of creating churches worth getting up for is the unleashing of those gifts that push us forward more aggressively and with some risk taking, some exploration outside our places of comfort. To stick with the taxonomy we've outlined so far, the recruiters/evangelists will often push us to engage in recruitment in new and different ways. They will recognize that the methods have to be contextualized to different situations—that a different generation will likely need to be reached in new ways fitted to them. They will remind us that the onus is on us to find new ways to be in mission to potential recruits, pushing us outside the comfort of attractional models we are used to. Initially, much of what they want us to do may sound strange and "different," but their empowerment by God for this leadership role means we need to listen, be open, and often follow into places we'd likely not go on our own.

Those with the gift of apostolicity will frequently cast visions that seem to us outrageous, obviously beyond our current abilities, clearly too risky, and too likely to fail. Our desire for safety will make it hard for us to submit ourselves to big dreams, and of course, the bigger the dream, the harder it will be. They will drive us crazy with their insistence that the old ways that worked so well simply will not work anymore. But, you know what? They'll often be right.

Finally, the prophets . . . well, they'll just drive us crazy on principle. They will often side with our critics, insisting that the criticisms they raise are more right than wrong. They'll have the audacity to pound their fists on the table and tell us that too many of the dominant presuppositions that drive our ministry are corrupted and need to be rethought. Prophets will speak God's truth to the systems of power that have arisen to shield us from the chaos, but in so doing have also blinded us to our own collusion with the systems of power in the culture around us. Those who seek safety often desire compromise for the sake of safety, but those who prophetically speak God's challenge to us will insist that the compromise costs too much. In short, those leadership types that fit into the overarching "growth/expansion" category will forever be urging us to do more, take more risks, get outside our comfort zones.

Balancing

Just as one can see how easily we might allow ourselves to become unbalanced in the direction of the maintenance roles, we can easily see how over-emphasizing the others will draw us out of balance in a different way. Those who recruit can become so occupied with numerical growth that they forget the need of teachers who will train new recruits to live the life of faith with integrity and persistence. When that happens, persons drop by the wayside just like those in the parable of the sower who sprouted quickly, but then withered. Too much attention on teaching and we find ourselves going years without any new recruits. Visionaries live for the next vision, the next "big thing." This is their gift, and thus it should be. But, if we do not balance visionaries with implementers, we will find ourselves ever chasing the "newest shiny ball" without ever getting to successful implementation. On the other hand, spending all the time on implementation for sure means stagnation. Finally, an imbalance in the direction of the prophetic voice will lead to discouragement for ministry partners, as the prophet is forever finding fault with the way things are. There is truth and value in their consistently pushing us toward repentance of our errors, but without balance, the prophet's voice becomes overly negative. In the end, then, prophets become isolated from the very ones who most need them. At the same time, setting the prophetic challenges aside means allowing the subtle idolatries that beset us to grow, like the weeds in the parable of the sower, until they choke out the life and witness of the church.

The obvious next question, then, is: How are we to balance the maintenance and the expansion/growth leadership roles in the church? Well, now, that's the $64,000 question, isn't it? Unfortunately, if figuring this out were an easy thing, we'd be doing a much better job of it. We would have a tool that would allow us to measure how we are doing and then make the necessary corrections. In a nutshell, the answer is that what constitutes the right balance of the different roles will be heavily context dependent. For example, different churches can process change at different rates. Some can move forward into a new vision for church rapidly, while others have long-established patterns that will require patience and persistence to overcome. Long-term success will not be served by simply ramming through change at rates that cannot be tolerated by our congregations. Instead, it will require wisdom and patience, both to discern the proper balance in specific situations and to determine a healthy rate of implementation of new paradigms. Step one is the willingness to admit the extent to which we have become imbalanced. Once that is firmly grasped, then we can begin to experiment with strategies that bring the missing leadership roles into place. The proof, as they say, will be in the pudding.

Given the overwhelming number of churches in the world that are small (under 100 parishioners), it will surely be the case that some churches will not be financially able to bear the burden of hiring folks with the differing skills. In those cases, we need to think about ways for churches to partner together to bring the appropriate balance of skills together. To work together in this way (dare I dream, even across denominational lines?) will serve two purposes. First, it will enable the rebalancing we may need even in the face of smallish budgets. This will help resolve the challenge we've discussed in this chapter. Second, though, it will begin to drive us away from our isolation as individual congregations and begin to force us to act more like the unified body that Christ Jesus envisions in his words to the earliest disciples. We are created in the image of a God who is Trinitarian first and foremost, which means we have been created for relationships. That applies, of course, to us as individual persons, but I would argue it also applies to us as individual congregations. Let the rebalancing and partnering begin!

Postscript on Risk Taking

The whole set of issues surrounding the role of risk taking in churches worth getting up for is both important and complicated enough to warrant extra attention. In fact, I had initially considered dedicating an entire chapter to the topic but finally decided to deal with it in what seems to be a natural postscript to this chapter on church leadership. As outlined above, risk taking is both necessary and, well, risky for the church. On the one hand, always avoiding risks, always taking the safer route, makes long-term stagnation, and perhaps death, likely. To take risks opens us up to the possibility that things will not go well, that the risk will blow up in our faces, and leave us in a crisis of one sort or another. Yet, visionary leaders are needed who will see new ways of doing things, new ways that are inherently risky just because they move away from the safe things that have worked in the past. At some point, the old ways no longer work, and to continue to push them beyond their usefulness is to invite decline in ministry effectiveness. Truly visionary leaders are those who think outside the box themselves as well as encourage and inspire those around them to do the same thing. In other words, these kinds of leaders, to be most effective, must both "dream dreams" and encourage the same in those around them.

Unfortunately, there are additional complications that arise regarding innovation and risk taking when one considers the ways in which religious leaders get implicated in the results produced by their churches and ministries. When high-profile religious leaders reach a point where their personal identities are closely intertwined with their church or ministry, the willingness to take risks, and especially to empower others to take risks, can quite easily become constrained, and somewhat understandably so. In these situations, the successes or failures of the ministries are often ascribed to that high-profile leader. To allow others, then, to take risks for the church or ministry is often seen by the leader as unnecessarily putting his or her personal future in the hands of staff. The reasoning seems to go something like this: Since the success or failure of this ministry is going to have such an impact on me personally, I should hold decision making on innovative and risky ideas close to the vest. At least, then, if I fail, it will be my own fault and not someone else's.

I think this is mostly mistaken and in fact counterproductive in many ways.

First, one has to wonder how healthy it is, particularly in church or ministry settings, to allow it to become the case that the leader is so closely and personally tied to the success of the church or ministry. While a dynamic leader can become a vital source of energy and support, we have always to remember that the head of the church, and of our parachurch ministries as well, is Jesus. Service to him is always to be the central issue for us. When we allow our own personal identities to get too intertwined with our ministry, then we have allowed the focus to be shifted from him to us. What we need to recall here is the attitude of John the Baptist, who, upon seeing Jesus, pointed to him and said, "He must increase, and I must decrease." It will not always be the case that the path that best points to Jesus will be the same one that best serves our personal interests. Is it the case that we might suffer personal harm because of ministry decisions not our own? Of course, but that's just the nature of ministry.

Second, no one person, no matter how smart or charismatic, has a corner on all the good ideas. Particularly effective visionary leaders are those who have a higher than normal proportion of good ideas, but even they are not always right. No matter how good and innovative the leader, we ought never to put all our ministry eggs in one basket. In fact, as we noted in the earlier sections of the chapter, it is not always the case that the leader of the church—the lead pastor, for example—will be the one who is most visionary. Part of the point of this chapter is that the role of visionary (as well as the other growth/expansion roles) is critical to the health of the church as are the other roles. No one person will have all the gifts, and the team in position to engage in discernment and ultimately to make decisions about moving on risky ideas must actively look for persons skilled in each area. In fact, in some cases, we may find multiple individuals with the different leadership skills. The high-profile leader who holds decision making too closely for fear of personal failure misses this important point.

Third, and closely related, unwillingness to delegate authority to "dream big" fails to take advantage of the inherent skills of the persons that leaders have recruited to their staffs. Nothing can be more disempowering than the leader who is intentional about recruiting the best people to a staff, only then to fail to utilize the gifts of these highly talented people. High staff turnover is often a sign of this particular failure of leadership. When the person in a leadership role invites and encourages those around him or her to offer their best ideas—no matter how radical; when the leader is receptive to the critiques of the staff, when the leader invests trust in people by empowering them to move forward with their dreams and ideas, that leader creates an environment of health and innovation. Will every idea turn out great? Of course not, but the effective leader takes failures in stride and recognizes them as part of the necessary fodder required both to develop a team and to lead the church to vibrancy.

Finally, one other reason high-profile leaders should resist this way of thinking about decision making with regard to innovation is, quite simply, the fact that they will not always be around. In other words, churches and ministries are generally intended to survive their leaders. By taking the time to encourage everyone to develop their skills to the fullest, by taking time to encourage creativity and innovation at all levels, leaders are preparing a ministry to be successful long after they are gone.

As an example of a healthy way to think about innovation and creativity in a church setting, I reference a motto used by Mike Slaughter to capture his leadership commitment at the church where he serves as lead pastor—Ginghamsburg United Methodist near Dayton, Ohio. He once said that at Ginghamsburg, they think about empowering folks by saying they operate with high expectations, high permissions, with permission to fail.

To conclude our discussion about risk taking in particular, but, frankly, about leadership in all the different ministry roles, let's explore the three different ideas embodied in in Mike's leadership motto.

High Expectations. I doubt that anyone who visits Ginghamsburg will walk away with any other conclusion but that Ginghamsburg has high expectations that all aspects of ministry will be executed with excellence. In fact, Mike Slaughter was one of the ones who during my interviews gave the most emphasis to the role of excellence in creating churches worth getting up for. High expectations can be communicated in many ways. While some seem to push for excellence through fear, through the threat of punishment for failure, I have found it more effective to push for excellence through encouragement. No one wants to fail and no one undertakes a project thinking they are going to fail. By exhibiting trust in a person's skills and intentions, I find that we consistently create better outcomes and a stronger sense of teamwork. At the same time, if we do not clearly communicate our expectations, we should not be surprised when that's not what we get. When it comes to new and innovative ministry opportunities, we must be clear that we are not just engaging in "trial and error," but that we are undertaking these outside-the-box ideas because we trust they will contribute to the ministry of the church.

High Permissions. When he says that he tries to lead with an attitude of "high permissions," Mike Slaughter means that he is intentional about encouraging staff and parishioners to pursue their dreams.

That does not mean that every idea brought forward is going to be pursued by the staff or that every single idea is going to receive funding. What it means is that when folks come to him with ideas for new or innovative ministries, he resists responding to them with "we can't afford it" or "we don't have the time." Instead, he encourages folks to figure out ways to take on the dreams they have—find volunteers to help staff it, find the money needed to make it viable. To embody a culture of high permissions is also to encourage a culture of innovation and creativity. Somehow, Ginghamsburg's high-profile pastor with a successful ministry has managed to encourage and allow creativity and risk taking, not overly worried that a particular ministry's failure will damage him personally.

With Permission to Fail. This may be the most important part of the triad. To communicate to your staff that they have "permission to fail" is to make explicit the fact that one recognizes that risk taking and innovation will include cases where things don't turn out as planned. There will be times when things fail. If folks sense a critical culture, where they are going to be criticized and looked down on for trying something new and failing, the natural outcome will be that folks won't try new things. They will opt for the safe, for the known, and, as we've noted several times in this chapter, that is to put things on the path to stagnation and decline. The path to churches worth getting up for necessarily goes right through innovation, right through creating new wineskins to hold the new wine. But, to recognize that and to be ready and willing to follow that path includes being ready to accept those cases where it doesn't turn out as expected. It also has to include permission to fail.

Risk taking, innovation, creativity in ministry: these are all scary, but essential aspects of churches that will be worth getting up for, not just today, but into the future. Figuring out how to manage both maintenance and expansion/growth, creating bridges that allow us to move from our current comfort to the next place God is leading us, is tricky and complicated. But, it is essential. May God grant us wisdom in the ongoing attempt to balance these two poles!

Chapter 6

Focus, Focus, Focus

I recall an episode of a popular television comedy. As one character is driving the other to work, the passenger berates the driver for not paying enough attention to her driverly duties. Her "check engine" light is on—why hasn't she taken care of that? She is not taking the route to work that the driver he usually rides with takes. Does she know where she is going? Besides, this particular route has many speed bumps—why would anyone want to drive this route anyway? And, she is speeding ten miles per hour over the posted speed limit. As he gives her a hard time over all the different ways in which she is not being sufficiently attentive, suddenly his head turns sharply to the right and he says, "Oh, look, a new putt-putt course!" It seems we all have trouble staying focused on the task at hand. It's just that different things distract us.

What about the church? Are we easily distracted from our core mission? While I think the opening story is a cute depiction of how easily we can find our attention turned from things more important to things vastly less important, I don't think the church is distracted from its mission so easily. Well, not *quite* that easily. Yet, one does have to wonder, on occasion, if we have forgotten that the main task of the church is to be the church, to be an outpost and a model of a new kingdom, a different way of living together. How can we be sure that the things we take on, the things to which we make commitments of time, talent, and resources, really are the right things, the best things? The potential for having our attention spread too broadly, so broadly that we might fail to be faithful stewards of our main tasks, was brought more into the center of my attention by some comments from Nadia Bolz-Weber.

In the course of our conversation about churches that are worth getting up for, she returned to the core issue: what makes a gathering of people the church rather than some other social institution? What is it that keeps church from being, oh, say, "the Elks Club with Eucharist?" was one colorful way she put it. Too easily, she mused, it seems Christians are distracted into producing bad knockoffs of things the culture does better. Why are we distracted into "knockoff production"? We see products or activities that already have a following, or more crassly, a market in the broader culture, so maybe we figure that if a given kind of thing or event is popular in the culture, why not provide a Christian version? You know, in order to leverage its popularity to draw attention to the church? Or, perhaps even to serve the somewhat more mundane goal of making money? Well, the problem, according to Bolz-Weber, is that we too often merely produce *poor* knockoffs, and our attempt to pander to market interests becomes quickly transparent. It becomes more of a turnoff. But, of course, that's not the only problem. Perhaps even more significant is that the time and energy we invest in producing poor imitations deplete us of critical energy needed to live out our role of being the church.

We could take the time to pause and name some of the items that Bolz-Weber gave as examples of things in which she felt the Christian subculture was engaged in "poor knockoff production." However, we need not get bogged down in a discussion about whether one should or should not agree with the particular list that came up in our discussion. Instead, we can come at it from the other end: What is unique about the things that churches offer to the cultures in which they are situated?

Since Bolz-Weber got us into this discussion, let's start with her answer to the question: What are the things, offered uniquely by the church, that make it the church? She identified three things:

1. The church is where the gospel/good news is preached.

2. The church is where the forgiveness of sins is proclaimed.

3. The church is where the sacraments are administered—baptism is performed and the Lord's Supper is served.[1]

If these are the unique things with which the church has been entrusted, the things that actually make the church the church, then we need to pause and consider each. Then we need to ask ourselves two questions: Are we doing these? If so, are we doing them well?

There is probably no other word associated with Christian faith that is more dreaded, by both Christians and non-Christians alike, than the word "evangelism." If you are a follower of Jesus, then "evangelism" often conjures up feelings of guilt and disquiet. Guilt arises because we fear we are not living up to the Great Commission's injunction to go and make disciples throughout all the world. We may genuinely believe that what we have to share is indeed good news. Yet, the idea of telling others of our faith—of the good news—and then inviting them to exercise faith for themselves brings back too many negative images as well as a fear of personal rejection. If people reject the good news, we feel they are rejecting us as well. And, indeed, they might well be.

Disquiet with spreading the gospel comes from recognizing the negative connotation that evangelism has with those around us. We suspect that even to begin to talk with our unchurched friends and neighbors in a way that has an evangelistic tone will merely turn them off and push them further away. We fear it will seem to be a rude intrusion of a topic foreign to them. Very few of us enjoy talking with another about a topic we know to be unpopular. Of course, many who are not followers of Jesus can imagine nothing worse than having someone try to convert them to religious faith. Politics and religion, we're told, are two topics not to be discussed in polite company, and evangelism is frequently seen as the most unpleasant of the already myriad of unpleasant religious topics. So, we often allow this set of feelings to keep us quiet. Yet, as Bolz-Weber rightly notes, surely the preaching of the good news is both unique to the church and central to its mission.

In this section, it may appear that I have shifted from discussing the importance of "preaching the gospel/good news" to a discussion on what might sound more like personal and corporate evangelism. However, as will become more evident in a moment, to engage in preaching the gospel/good news is to engage in evangelism. Perhaps we should take a step back and look at this from a different perspective. We should begin with a deeper look at what constitutes the good news, or the gospel.

The Good News

I will not bog the reader down in a lot of analysis of Greek, but it is important to look at the word we translate into English as *evangelism*. Looking at that Greek word will make it immediately obvious how close the two words are in appearance. If we simply transliterate[2] the word, we get: *euangellion*. You can immediately see the similarity between the words *evangelism* and *euangellion*. The latter can be broken down further to make the meaning clearer. It is comprised of a prefix: *eu,* and a stem: *angellion.* Right away we notice that the stem has the English word *angel* at its core. We all know what an angel is, a supernatural creature initially created to serve God. In Greek, the term that corresponds to *angel (angelos)* carries the primary meaning of messenger; that is, the term "angel" speaks of a creature who serves God as a messenger. Originally, the term could reference a human or a supernatural messenger. (So, the root meaning of *angelos* is that of messenger, one sent with a particular message.) When the word becomes *angellion*, the root meaning is the message or announcement that the *angelos* has been sent to deliver. The prefix to *angellion, eu,* carries with it the meaning *good.* The basic idea that the English term *evangelism* carries over with it from the original Greek term *euangellion,* particularly as it is used in the New Testament, is the idea of an announcement or message from God, the content of which is *good.* To engage in evangelism, then, is to engage in preaching a message with content that is a good announcement from God. Eventually, in Anglo-Saxon, the phrase became "glad tidings" or "good news" and took the form *Godspell*, eventually shortened to our contemporary term *gospel*. Evangelism, then, is the task of announcing, or preaching, good news to those around us.

I expect we can do no better than Jesus' own words when it comes to providing a definition for the good news. Consider, for example, Luke 4:18-19 (reading from the Book of Isaiah):

> The Spirit of the Lord is upon me, because the Lord has anointed me. He has sent me to preach good news to the poor, to proclaim release to the prisoners and recovery of sight to the blind, to liberate the oppressed, and to proclaim the year of the Lord's favor.

There is some debate on how to read this. For example, the New Testament Greek professor with whom I studied suggested that "good news to the poor" is a summary phrase and that the next three clauses are examples of what it means to preach good news to the poor. What can cause folks to be poor in the first place? Well, those who have been imprisoned are often those who are from poorer socioeconomic classes. And of course, prisoners cannot provide for their families while imprisoned. Similarly, those in bad health (in this case in Scripture, blind) were the ones who often ended up as poor beggars. Those who are oppressed and exploited, likewise, often end up poor and marginalized. In this reading, what does it mean to preach good news to the poor? Well, it means to preach release to those imprisoned, to heal those who cannot see, and to remove the bonds of oppression from those exploited. However we read this passage, though, it is important to note that in this passage, often taken as Jesus' "mission statement," good news is good news *to the poor*—a thing we ought not overlook as we ponder the implications of being a church that has as its primary focus the proclamation of the good news. And, in the proclaiming of the good news, we must remember that "The Gospel is not an empty word; it is effective power which brings to pass what it says because God is its author."[3]

Perhaps someone will want to argue that the first two points raised by Bolz-Weber are really the same thing. What can be better "good news" than hearing the proclamation of the forgiveness of sins? But, that collapses things too quickly, doesn't it? If we make "good news" synonymous with the forgiveness of sins, the task of actually making better the circumstances in which folks find themselves is easily lost. Besides, in the passage above, regardless of how you take it, the focus is on concrete and visible actions—the prisoners are released, blind folks are made to see, those exploited and oppressed are freed. That is not to deny that the passage also has a spiritual dimension, but rather it is to make sure that we do not overlook the concrete actions required from us as followers of Jesus.

To focus, however, on the proclamation of the forgiveness of sins is to move increasingly to the spiritual dimension of ourselves.[4] Let us delve more deeply into what it means for the church to proclaim the forgiveness of sins.

The Forgiveness of Sins

One of my favorite passages of Scripture is Romans 5:8, which reminds us that the overwhelming love of God is demonstrated by the fact that *while we were yet sinners*, Christ died for us. To use language from the historical doctrines of the church, Christ's death accomplished the atonement for human sins. Human sin is the basis for the alienation that we experience between us and our fellow humans and the alienation we experience between ourselves and God. Sin is constituted by acts that create alienation through damaging what would otherwise be healthy relationships between humans and between humans and God. Just to give a few examples, God is the Creator of humanity and as such is due our love and respect. When we fail to honor God as Creator, we alienate ourselves from God by attempting to think of ourselves in relationship to God in ways that are not based on a right understanding of our respective places. God has created us for relationships of mutual interdependence with other humans around us that are based on mutual respect, love, and integrity. When we conduct ourselves in our relationships with others in ways that do not embody those characteristics, we alienate ourselves from each other. Specific behaviors that create such alienation include lying, cheating, stealing, or doing physical harm to each other. These are rightly called sins to the extent they become a force of alienation among us and between us and God.

When we say that what Jesus accomplished was the forgiveness of sins, we are saying that the sacrifice of himself, his letting the powers of darkness do their worst to him, his death on the cross were means that God used to make the restoration of right relationships possible. Within the history of the broader Christian tradition, there have been different ways to understand what happened in the atonement, different ways of seeing how Christ's death accomplished the restoration of right relationships. However, what has been agreed is that the path to overcoming the alienating effects of sin was established and that God's mighty work of reconciliation has reached its apex. God has declared our sins forgiven; that is, *atonement* has been made for our sins, and all the steps on God's side needed to repair the breach have been made. The message, "Atonement has been made!" makes evident to us that the work of Christ has accomplished its intended ends: God has forgiven our sins and all that remains is for us to appropriate that forgiveness.

So, in addition to proclaiming the good news in the sense we discussed earlier, the church is the place uniquely chosen by God to proclaim the forgiveness of sins. We have been tasked to tell the world that God has done all that is necessary from God's side to solve the vexing problem of alienation—alienation from God, alienation from others, even self-alienation. We live in a culture in which the notion of sin often is seen problematically, and it may take some time for us to recapture the meaning the term carries in Scripture. Or, perhaps what we need to do is couch discussions of sin in terms that focus less on condemnation and more on the relational character of sin and, thus, why God cares so much about it. Sometimes we Christians can become overly abstract in our discussions of sin, making it sound like God is the cosmic killjoy, rather than properly identifying the corrosive and damaging effects of sin to our relationships with others.

Let me share a story once told to me. My friend, a follower of Jesus, was being asked by another person, not a follower of Jesus, why it was that the Christian God was so interested in stopping things that humans might take to be fun. The person brought up the Ten Commandments and asked why, for example, it was that God cared with whom she might have sex. My friend responded something like this:

I think you are reading those commandments in the wrong way. Let me tell you how I read them. God says to us: "I have created you for deep, personal relationships of trust and mutuality. If you lie to each other, it destroys trust. So, don't lie to each other. The relationships that I intend cannot exist in a context where you steal from each other. So, don't steal. And, I know how powerful sexual encounters are. I created them, after all. But, if you are not careful, if you betray your spouse, you will be set on a path to be consumed by your lusts. So, don't commit adultery."

You can see the point. My friend was trying to show how the commandments were not constructed by God as some abstract way to limit things we might want to do. Instead, they were put in place because God knows how we were created to be and what fuels that way of being. The various commandments to us are aimed to make that way of living together not only possible, but normative.

Whether or not a person has a strong appreciation for the Christian doctrine of sin, I think that we all have an implicit sense that something is not right, that our relationships are *off*, that something needs to be fixed. We Christians believe we know both the underlying cause of this alienation as well as the solution for it.

Rather than focus on the negative consequences of sin (not because they are unimportant, but because, as I just said, we have at least an *implicit* sense that something is wrong), let us embrace that unique role of the church to proclaim the forgiveness of sins. Let us be agents of reconciliation. Let us be ones who tell and retell the parable of the prodigal son (or, as some prefer, the parable of a father's prodigal love), reminding folks that God's love is so great that God stands not only ready, but eager to receive all who wish to take advantage of that forgiveness. When we are reminded of the need to focus our ministries, let us not lose sight of the importance of that unique and critical task to which God has assigned the church: let us be bold in our proclamation of the forgiveness of sins!

The Eucharist

We now come to the third of the three unique and critical tasks of the church that we named at the oustet: the serving of the Eucharist. Within different traditions, we tend to focus on different terms to describe the Eucharist—in some, we call it Communion, and in others, the Lord's Supper.[5] All three communicate important aspects of what's going on in this most Christian of Christian sacraments. The term "Eucharist," as the reader has probably guessed, is also a term that has been pretty directly transliterated from Greek to English. Upon first glance, the reader might expect the term to be divided into the prefix *eu* attached to the stem *charist* or some such, but as it turns out, this is not the case.[6] Instead, the Greek word from which we get the term "Eucharist" is actually a family of words that are translated as different forms of the word "prayer," and other related ideas. More specifically, in 1 Corinthians 11:24, the term is translated as "thanksgiving." In the second term, "Communion," we have a word that comes from the Latin *communio*, which means a sharing in common. As one can see, the whole family of words relating to the term "community" also arises from this root. Finally, some traditions describe the sacrament more descriptively by calling it the "Lord's Supper." Something critical to understanding the nature of what is happening in the sacrament of sharing bread and wine/juice is brought by each name.

From "Eucharist," we are reminded that the common meal is a meal of celebration, one in which we both explicitly and implicitly offer our thanks to God for the sacrifice of Christ which the meal commemorates. From "Communion," our attention is drawn to the communal nature of sacrament. It is not something that we celebrate on our own, but rather a community event where God's children gather together to form the community united by their allegiance to Christ. Finally, from "the Lord's Supper," we are reminded that we unite at the invitation of the one who is our Lord—not just our Lord, in fact, but as Paul reminds us, Lord of all. In the sharing of the bread and the wine/juice, in the participation in this sacrament of the Christian faith, we put our individuality behind us and we take up our place alongside others who have committed themselves to God as the community of God, a people united in commitment to Jesus, a community gathered to give thanks for all that God, in Christ, has done for us. From the different names we use to describe the sacrament, we gather these things. But more reflection is appropriate before we move on.

Sharing table fellowship (in short, eating together) is a common way of expressing hospitality and friendship across a wide variety of cultures. There is an air of acceptance, vulnerability, and intimacy that is evident when we gather around a table to share a common meal. We do not invite those to eat with us unless they are friends or ones with whom we wish to establish friendship. Since God is the initiator of the Eucharist, it is worth stopping to ponder the implications—specifically that God considers us friends. Perhaps the term "friend" has become too tame in our contemporary culture to convey the depth we need for our discussion here. Perhaps not. To recognize, however, the unique and critical role of the church to serve this sacrament is to recognize that God has empowered us to welcome others to the table as friends of God. Imagine getting a fancy and elegant invitation in the mail. In the upper, left-hand corner, the place reserved for the return address, we see the embossed symbol for the White House. When we open it, we find that the president of the United States has invited us to join him for a state dinner, a special event at which the president himself will be present. For most, this would be a great honor, whether or not the president happened to share our beliefs and commitments. Well, when the church rallies those present around the Communion rail, we are receiving an invitation of even greater import, for not the president of the United States, but God Almighty, the Creator of all, is the one who invites and gathers us. We are invited to be the friends of God!

Implicit, of course, in the invitation to be friends of God is the recognition that in calling us around the table, united by our allegiance to Christ, all those who gather with us are our family, our community. The call to the table carries with it the invitation to go forth from it, committed to live in peace and harmony with God and our fellow humans. We are called into existence as the people of God, sisters and brothers to each other and children of God. In the gathering, the church both announces and embodies the unity of all under the lordship of Christ. Let us not gather around the table oblivious to the deeper meaning, but rather let us approach with "eyes wide open," embracing the offer of God's friendship and embodying the community into which we are being formed.

Embody and Proclaim These Three

In this chapter, I intentionally began with the focus around the proclamation of good news because, in a sense, all three of the places that Bolz-Weber suggested the church ought rightly focus its attention are really, really good news. In the first case, we announce explicitly the concrete reality of the good news in all its physical and spiritual reality. In the second, we announce the good news of the forgiveness of sins, the good news that the stifling alienation has been overcome through the sacrifice of Christ. While the appropriation of the effects and consequences of that forgiveness awaits our response, it has already been accomplished, now and forever. Finally, this new community being called into being around Christ and under allegiance to him is also called to join together, around the table, as friends of God and of each other, to break bread and share fellowship. Again, it is good news, through and through.

Is it the case that churches undertake other activities? Most certainly. Is it the case that this engagement in other activities can be a good thing? Yes, it is the case. However, these three things are uniquely given to the church to embody and proclaim. Whatever else we do, we cannot lose sight of these three. They are the things that persons can get nowhere else except in the church and they are all critically important to our well-being, physically, spiritually, and in every other way. Churches worth getting up for are those who fully embrace their task to proclaim good news, proclaim the forgiveness of sins, and unite under the banner of Christ in order to share the sacrament of Eucharist.

Chapter 7

Right Belief, Right Practice: Equal Partners?

There are hardly any who would deny the importance to the Christian faith of both right belief (orthodoxy) and right practice (orthopraxy). Perhaps there are a few who exist at the far extremes of this dichotomy—some who think that what one does matters not, as long as one believes the right things; and some who think that what one believes matters not, as long as one does the right things. However, for the most part, Christians agree that belief *and* practice matter and most churches at least try to pay attention to both. When there is disagreement on the roles of orthodoxy and orthopraxy, agreement tends to break down in a couple of different places. One point of contention relates to how we define the terms—what exactly do we mean by "right belief" and "right practice"?[1]

In some cases, right belief is taken in a very broad sense. Those holding this view would say that one believes rightly from a Christian perspective only if one correctly affirms every point the Bible teaches.[2] Others would connect right belief with affirmation of the Great Ecumenical Creeds, recognizing that legitimate debate exists as to what Scripture teaches on some issues. Yet others would set the bar lower for defining what constitutes the critical beliefs one must affirm in order to be Christian. Then, of course, there is the debate about what constitutes "right practice." Options here would be similar in kind to the ones involving right belief. Those on the more rigorous end would focus a great deal of attention on the claim that Jesus models for us, in virtually all that he does, the life that pleases God. Living rightly, then, engaging in the right sort of practices, would be to imitate Jesus in every way possible. Other Christians might agree in general that Jesus is our moral exemplar, but not feel that the phrase "imitation of Jesus" captures what right practice means. Yet others would not put much emphasis on the imitation of Jesus at all, for a variety of reasons.

The second point has to do with the relative emphasis each is given. Do we put right practice at the forefront? Or, do we make it a supplement to right belief? In other words, which is more important and to what extent ought one or the other be prioritized? Churches that focus on right belief draw attention to the statements or *propositions* that we believe. Propositions that are often made central to believing rightly as a Christian include the affirmations contained in the classic creeds and might include:

1. God's nature is Trinitarian, existing as Father, Son, and Holy Spirit.

2. Jesus was fully God and fully human.

3. The Bible is the inspired Word of God.

4. The death of Jesus on the cross makes atonement for human sin.

Those who put the primary emphasis on right belief generally do so arguing that too much attention on right practices underemphasizes God's grace and begins to make our right relationship with God too much about our works. That is, the claim is that too much attention on what we *do* begins to move from salvation by faith to salvation by works. So, churches that focus on right belief tend to put primary attention to our mental assent to the propositions that constitute orthodoxy. The primary work of the church, then, becomes spreading right belief and using evangelism as a tool to bring others into a position such that they concur with orthodox doctrine.

On the other hand, churches that focus on right practice draw our attention to the things that we do in order to live out the life of faith. These churches are particularly interested in the ways in which we are engaged missionally with those around us, those poor or otherwise on the margins especially. Those who put the primary emphasis on right practice will cite such passages as in James where we are told that even the demons believe and that faith (or right belief) without actions means little.[3] Churches that focus on right practices focus on missional activity, including such questions as:

1. How are we advocating for the poor and marginalized around us?

2. Are we faithfully imitating Jesus in the ways in which we engage those around us?

3. In particular, are we helping to meet the physical needs as well as the spiritual needs of those on the margins?

Those who place primary emphasis on right practice are quick to point out the physical expressions of the coming reign of God as embodied in Jesus' own preaching, say, for example, from his reading in the synagogue as recorded in Luke 4. The primary work of the church, according to those who see the faith this way, is the missional engagement with the world—in our local areas as well as around the world. They measure our faithfulness not primarily by what we believe, but by how well we embody the new way of being that is captured in the gospel. As we can see, while two different churches might agree that both right belief and right practice are, *in theory,* both very important, how that gets implemented at the local church level can vary a great deal. So, who is right? The "church as right belief" gang or the "church as right practice" gang? Well, honestly, both are, aren't they?

Uniting Right Belief and Right Practices

In their book *Churches That Make a Difference,* Ron Sider, Philip Olson, and Heidi Unruh argue that churches that are making a difference are ones that are increasingly characterized by what they call "holistic ministry." By holistic ministry, the authors mean ministry that faithfully unites both the concern about right belief and the concern about right practice. The subtitle helps to make the point: *Reaching Your Community with Good News and Good Works.* Early in the book, they make the point:

> The twentieth century saw a divisive argument between social gospel churches that focused one-sidedly on social action, and evangelistic churches that insisted that leading people to Christ was the only truly important mission of the church. The tragic results of that long argument have not entirely disappeared, but we have made great progress. Evangelical leaders today widely agree that biblical churches must combine word and deed, doing both evangelism and social ministry. Scores of historic evangelical congregations that focused almost exclusively on evangelism twenty years ago are now immersed in social engagement—without losing their evangelistic passion. Thousands of grassroots holistic ministries have emerged. Based on a national survey, sociologist Chris Smith concluded recently that "evangelicals may be the most committed carriers of a new Social Gospel." At the same time, mainline denominations have been engaged in conversations about the importance of evangelism. To an increasing degree, the church in America is ready to embark on a vast expansion of holistic ministry.[4]

I want to argue that churches that are worth getting up for are, in fact, churches that are making a difference in the communities where they are located. Sider and his coauthors agree that those churches are the ones that have and are learning to unite right belief and right practice.

Unfortunately, reaching proper balance in what these authors call "holistic ministry" is a difficult proposition as we can see from the continuing tendency of churches to overemphasize one side or the other. All this invites the question: What might proper balance look like? To answer that, let's take a look at a couple of the churches we've discussed along the way.

Mike Slaughter is, at core, an evangelical who is committed to traditional orthodoxy as regards Christian belief. He would affirm the classical creeds that express the Trinitarian nature of God, the dual nature of Jesus (both human and divine), as well as the basic contours of human atonement through the death of Christ. The church where he ministers calls individuals to personal faith in Christ and his preaching consistently emphasizes the traditional Protestant doctrine of salvation by faith. In short, his church consistently draws the congregation to what has been broadly accepted as the core beliefs of the Christian faith.

However, the church's ministry does not stop there. Several years back, Slaughter preached a sermon series entitled Christmas Is Not Your Birthday.[5] The series had as its goal two things. First, he wanted to remind his congregation that we have allowed commercialism and materialism to invade what is supposed to be the celebration of the birth of Jesus. In short, we treat it as if it were our birthday, with all the attendant gifts. Second, he identified a specific way in which the church could transform the self-centered materialism of Christmas into an opportunity to engage in missions. He did that by challenging the congregation of Ginghamsburg UMC to make a gift to the church during the Advent season, *equal to the sum of all the gifts they gave to family and friends for Christmas.* That money was not earmarked for local ministries (thus, making sure the gift did not end up being self-serving), but rather was designated for missions in the African nation of Darfur. Over the course of the last several years, GUMC has raised millions of dollars for ministry in Darfur. They have helped provide tens of thousands of sources for clean water, for example. Beyond the international work with Darfur, the church has taken on a number of missional projects in their local area, including partnering with churches in a poorer section of town, providing support for folks working on a GED, and helping with counseling services for those who would not otherwise be able to access them. Here, we see a good model of holistic ministry.

We could explore other examples, perhaps returning to Chris Seay and Ekklesia Church. In an earlier chapter, we discussed the radical hospitality the folks of Ekklesia seek to embody, both welcoming those on the margins and building bridges. Perhaps we could explore the ministry of Ros Picardo and Embrace Church in Lexington, Kentucky, a church with two campuses. One is located in the downtown area and is particularly welcoming to those who are on the margins for one reason or another; the other is located on the north side of town, in one of the poorer sections of town. Or, we could explore one of the several churches Sider, Olson, and Unruh explore in *Churches That Make a Difference,* churches that engage in a variety of outreach and advocacy missions. These are good examples of churches that combine a commitment to right belief and evangelism as well as missional outreach in their local communities and beyond.

Let me be clear: While there are indicators that we are living in a time of transition, it has been the case that we evangelicals have tended to focus much more on right belief than we have on right practice. This is particularly the case when we consider right practice beyond the limits of our own personal, internal practices of piety. We have allowed ourselves to focus too narrowly on right belief, and I argue that we need to recover a much stronger balance between the two. Just as we evangelicals have tended to be overly focused on right belief, many mainline denominations have been overly focused on right practice. I do not argue for a swing of the pendulum to the opposite side either for evangelicals or mainliners. Instead, we must come to a point of balance, recognizing that how we take on the task of missional engagement, imitating the model of Jesus, is just as, but not more, important as the propositions we believe about the Christian faith. Churches that are worth getting up for focus on both internal transformation of individuals and the external transformation of the cultures of which we are a part.

While we are exploring the relationship between right belief and right practice, there is another point that is worth our attention as we consider factors that may help make churches worth getting up for. In a conversation with Alan Hirsch, he raised the question: Are we spending too much time worrying about heresy and faulty belief? Again, a word of caution is necessary. Hirsch is *not* suggesting that there is no such thing as heresy, nor is he saying we should ignore it. What he is asking is: Have we expanded the number of beliefs that constitute "the essential beliefs of the Christian faith" to the point that we are creating obstacles to becoming followers of Jesus? Let's look at a couple of contrasts to make the point.

Are Obstacles Being Created?

It is quite easy for the beliefs we identify as critical to the Christian faith to grow to the point that they become oppressive. If someone were to ask "What are the beliefs one must hold to be a Christian?" how would you answer? I expect most would include statements about the nature of God, about the person and work of Jesus, and about the role the sacrifice of Jesus plays in making atonement for our sins. But, would you include statements about the nature of the church? About church hierarchy? That is, does a person have to see the church in a particular way to be Christian? Or be a member of a particular tradition/denomination? What about how one sees the role of the Bible in Christian faith? Is there a particular position regarding Scripture that one must hold or risk not being in right relationship with God? We can extend this to a wide range of questions about beliefs on a wide range of things. But there is no need to get into them all to make the point that we often create stumbling blocks for followers of Jesus by imposing requirements regarding certain beliefs that extend beyond where they should. Before we say more, let's take a little detour through the early church, a detour that Hirsch took me on as we discussed this topic.

In the course of our discussion, Hirsch used the apostle Paul as an example and made the following observations. After his conversion and personal study and preparation, Paul launched a number of missionary journeys. In the different cases, he would enter a new town and begin to engage folks about Jesus, bearing witness to the good news of the life, death, and resurrection of Jesus. In some cases (say, Corinth), Paul spent an extended time in the city, teaching, preaching, and helping the fledgling church to grow. In other cases, though, he spent relatively short periods in a given location—perhaps a few weeks, perhaps a bit more than a month. Then, he moved on to the next city, repeating and reproducing followers of Jesus wherever he went. After this relatively short period of time, Paul moved on to the next town, considering a new church to have been planted. This new church was largely on its own, no doubt under the leadership of folks who had been empowered by Paul to function in a leadership role. He might revisit the town at some point and certainly remained in contact with many communities through written correspondence. However, these newly established communities were allowed to move on with minimal oversight and, as Hirsch points out, largely seemed to move the mission of Jesus forward despite the relatively minimal teaching in Christian doctrine. There seemed to be an implicit degree of confidence in the ability of the Holy Spirit to lead these fledgling churches.

Now, this is another one of those places where I have to stop for a bit of caution and nuance. I can understand how some might begin to feel a bit nervous at the direction of the conversation. After all, and as we noted earlier, there are those who would argue that beliefs largely do not matter, that doctrine has become more a source of division than a help. But, I want to be crystal clear that this is not my position. I am trained as a systematic theologian, and as such, I am committed to the position that the core beliefs of the Christian faith are critically important. I have argued elsewhere that the early church's move to establish doctrinal standards was a necessary step. However, one need not devolve to the position that beliefs do not matter at all to be able to say that we can easily move to positions that tend to make normative beliefs that extend well beyond those that have been considered essential by large swaths of the historical Christian tradition. In the earliest church period, there was relatively little attention given to formal doctrinal beliefs. As the church was faced with different challenges, it rightly took up the challenge and developed creeds to capture the essential beliefs of the faith. They recognized that right belief mattered, and they took the steps necessary to identify them. Yet, we ought to recognize the wisdom of the church in leaving a large number of issues open for individual believers to decide on their own. Did the death of Christ atone for human sin? Yes, but the church let stand different theories about how. We could multiply examples.

Perhaps one way to capture the point is to say that during the New Testament and during the earliest church period, the focus was on putting faith *in* Jesus, not in the abstract beliefs that folks held *about* Jesus. Belief in Jesus was supposed to be transformative; it signaled a change of allegiance from one kingdom to another. Christian faith did not aim to leave humans living their lives, largely unchanged with regard to day-to-day practices with only a layer of beliefs about Jesus added on. It was about a belief in Jesus that radically turned upside down the way we Christians lived our day-to-day lives. What Hirsch wants us to see is that much of contemporary evangelicalism has turned inward, worried much more about right belief than right practice. He suggests that we rethink that, embracing the doctrinal core of the faith[6] without allowing ourselves to convert our own particular beliefs into a list of normative beliefs for all Christians.

Let me summarize the points of this chapter. First, this chapter has argued that both right belief and right practice matter, and I've expressed concern with the extent to which Protestantism has frequently divided along these lines—one side underemphasizing right practice and the other side underemphasizing right belief. Second, our focus on right belief is critically important. Yet, the temptation to make personal conclusions on an array of doctrinal beliefs normative, while understandable, must be avoided. Perhaps another read through the New Testament, with an eye to the expectations extended toward new Christians, might be particularly helpful. Third, those things that do constitute the core of the Christian faith must issue forth in transformation—at the personal level as well as at the level of our shared common lives. Those core beliefs should, in short, change the world.

Chapter 8

Moving beyond the Sacred/Secular Distinction

Some thirty years ago, *Mork and Mindy* was a popular comedy show. Mork was an alien from the planet Ork and Mindy was the kind earthling who had befriended him. During one episode, Mork was confronted with his first exposure to a pregnant human. On Ork, offspring arrived by rather different means, so the fact that a woman was "great with child" caused Mork some consternation at first. Mindy explained that the woman was pregnant, but that meant little to Mork. So, she simply told him that there was a baby inside. Mork got the most perplexed look on his face as he declared, "Oh my, kids do get in the darnedest places!" Well, you know what? If you take a look at how churches are developing in different parts of the country today, you might find yourself with a parallel sentiment: "Oh my, churches do get into the darnedest places!"

Think I'm joking? Think back 50 years or so. Who would have thought churches would be renting public schools for church services? Or, how many would have predicted that churches would have taken up residence in strip-mall, typically storefront, locations? Or, what about those who use movie theaters for a meeting place?[1] Or, who would have foreseen "cowboy churches" that meet in rural settings such as a barn or a rodeo arena? Oh, and those cowboy barns? Baptisms can occur in the stock tank normally used to provide drinking water for the animals. I am part of a congregation that has regular, informal services in (gasp!) a local bar once a month. Yes, indeed, churches are being found in the darnedest places!

But, is any of this a bad thing? For being baptized in Jesus, who was born in a manger, can you really imagine a better place than a stock tank? We live in an age when many have been burned or have become burned out on trying to look religious, a time when many are turned off just by the appearance of church. In these conditions, we have to seriously consider establishing churches and church-like services in what might be called "nontraditional" locations. I should be clear. The goal here is *not* to reduce the beliefs and obligations that attend Christian faith, but rather to demonstrate that some of the normal, more formal trappings of the church are matters of *preference* and not matters essential to the Christian faith. Matters of preference still make a difference, though, and no one is arguing to move away from the form church has traditionally taken altogether. The goal is to create church contexts and environments that remove obstacles to participation and that make folks with differing preferences feel welcome. In other words, one can be the church and do church services in a warehouse in the artsy center of town[2] or in a downtown movie theater[3] or in buildings that have become run-down and dilapidated.[4] To borrow an old idea, the church is not the building, but rather the people who make up the community and mission of the church.

I believe that the fact that churches are showing up in the darnedest places is an enormously positive statement about the outreach of the contemporary church. As we have seen in other chapters, a wide variety of things about the contemporary church and church folk rightly cause us consternation. This trend of nontraditional locations with folks engaged in nontraditional worship and small group meetings, however, is something we should rejoice in and encourage. This trend carries with it implications that extend in at least a couple of different directions that each have significance for the church.

The Church Getting Outside Itself—the Missional Church

In the first place, and along the lines we've discussed so far, more frequent utilization of nontraditional venues and formats for church represents an encouraging willingness on the part of the church to get outside itself. The church has far too frequently allowed itself to rest behind the comfort of its four walls and extend invitations to those on the outside to come to us. Consistent with contemporary language, we called this way of doing church an "attractional model." That is, our goal is to *attract* folks to us. However, we serve a Lord who modeled for us what it means to be in mission. Scripture tells us that God *sent* Jesus to us to rescue us from our sins. God did not sit passively by, waiting for us to return to him. Rather, in the words of Romans 5:6-10, while we were still sinners,[5] Christ was sent and died for us. Even though we were the ones who had sinned, even though the relationship between God and humanity was breached from the human side, God took the initiative to be *in mission* to us by sending Jesus. The missional church movement has encouraged us to remember that being faithful to the Christian calling to be imitators of God makes it necessary for us to look at ways we are going to "go out" in mission to those around us. We should all applaud churches that are using and exploring nontraditional locations and formats. In going beyond our comfort zone in this way, we imitate our Lord.

Another aspect of this same point comes into view when we recognize and admit that the church has not always been the most welcoming place. The reason some folks have given up on church is because of the bad experiences they have had there—bad experiences, possibly from their youth, that still haunt them today. Is it the case that everyone who leaves the church does so because of flaws or mistakes on the church's part? Of course not, but there are too many who fall into that category. Perhaps all of us have heard of churches that self-identify as places that are safe and welcoming to those who have been burned or hurt in some way by the church. If we want to dig into this in more detail, if we wish to explore the different ways in which folks feel let down by the church, I recommend reading David Kinnaman's *You Lost Me: Why Young Christians Are Leaving Church . . . and Rethinking Faith.* In *unChristian*, Kinnaman explores attitudes toward Christian faith. In *You Lost Me*, he explores the reasons why the 16–29 demographic is walking away from traditional churches and thinking about Christian faith in new ways. The book is relevant to the discussion here in that it identifies the kind of hurts that the church has inflicted (and, sadly, often continues to inflict) on those who attend.

By moving to nontraditional venues and formats, we at least implicitly admit that church does not have to be done as it frequently has been. Rather than insisting that those outside come in and get comfortable with what we are already doing, those who engage in the trends we are discussing in this chapter have decided that they have to leave their comfort zones and be willing to participate in ways that feel more comfortable to the ones with whom we wish to engage. And, to those who feel that church has let them down in the past, our attempt to reach them on their "home turf" demonstrates a willingness to take the first step in correcting those past wrongs, even in those cases where the wrongs were not created by us specifically.

Sacred Versus Secular

The last few paragraphs all fall under the general heading of missional church, the recognition that we in the church need to be fully engaged in the task of going out to be in mission to those around us. I want to move now to a second implication of the trend to move into nontraditional spaces and formats: what it implies for the ministry of the church and how it helps to create churches worth getting up for. Deb Hirsch[6] brought this to my attention during our discussion on the themes of this book. She commented on how, when she and her husband, Al, took over the leadership of a particular church they served, they immediately began to make the place more "normal." They replaced the pews with couches, round tables with chairs, and other furniture that gave the worship space a more "homey" feel. It was, of course, a switch from an environment that has been tradition-ally associated with church (rows of pews, all facing forward toward where the "show" is conducted) to something less formal and more inviting. The couches gave folks a comfortable place to sit while they chatted and awaited the start of the service. The round tables placed people in chairs so that they faced each other during preliminaries to the service and accommodated discussion after the service, allowing folks to hang around and discuss the different points that came up during the service.

This move away from the traditional pew format to one very differ-ent, one intended to send different kinds of messages, carries with it an underlying theological commitment that is, I believe, critically impor-tant for the day in which we live. What the Hirsches were trying to do as they changed the common furniture for their worship gatherings was to begin to *erase the wall between the sacred and the secular*. Let me begin by saying a little about what this means before we get into why it matters. A common way to think about the term "sacred" is to say that something is sacred because it is in some way associated with God. The thing that we identify as sacred has been or is to be used for reli-gious purposes. We speak, for example, of baptism and Communion as sacred rites. Likewise, the whole of a worship service can be character-ized as a sacred rite (or, perhaps more accurately, a series of sacred rites conducted together). So, a thing is sacred to the extent it is set apart or dedicated to religious purposes. A second common way to think of the sacred is to put it over against or in opposition to the secular. A thing is "secular" to the extent it does *not* have a particular religious use or practice, to the extent it is not associated with God.

In our everyday lives, I think we do tend to think of the sacred and the secular as standing opposite to each other. Perhaps the thing we most explicitly associate with the idea of sacredness is the weekly worship service. It is the epitome of the sacred in that it is the period of time that we explicitly set aside in order to gather in a special place to engage in acts of worship and piety. When we think of it this way, it is natural to think of the time in which we do this as sacred time. Likewise, we naturally think of the space in which we worship as sacred space. Following the reasoning logically to its conclusion, we want to take steps that exemplify both the sacredness of the time and the sacredness of the space. We draw attention to the commandment about Sabbath observance as a way to show that God infused the sacred time with special significance when that observance was made the subject of one of the Ten Commandments. Similarly, in the Hebrew Bible, we see God giving instructions for the creation of special spaces in which the sacred rites would be conducted. Granted, those sacred rites are very different than the ones we practice today, but the point is still the same: when God commanded the observance of special times, instructions were also given for the sacred spaces in which the sacred practices would be undertaken. Well, this all makes sense, right? So, why would Deb Hirsch want to erase the distinction between the sacred and the secular? And, why am I affirming the move in that direction? I'm glad you asked.

Let me begin my answer with a question: Is it really the case that, from a Christian standpoint, there is any space or time that is not related to God? I think that what we as Christians would want to say is that if secular means apart from God, then there is no secular space and all is sacred. Let me say that again. If identifying a space as secular means to identify a space as not being intimately connected to God, then as Christians, we have to deny the existence of secular space or time or anything. I am not sure that the initial intent of the creation of particular times and spaces for worship was to set up a dichotomy that divided the world into sacred and secular. Rather, if we look at the biblical narratives, I believe that we end up with a sense that *all* time and space belongs to and is intimately related to God. The creation of particular times and spaces for observance of sacred rites was not intended to divide sacred from secular, but rather to identify for us periods and spaces of particular focus on God. Perhaps I am reading optimistically in drawing these conclusions, but even if so, I would argue that we Christians are much more interested in seeing all spaces and times infused with the holiness of the sacred.

The steps the Hirsches were taking to make the worship space seem more "normal" were intended to communicate to folks the sacredness of all space. When at home on the couch, we should no less feel we are in God's presence than when we sit on the couch in worship. When we are gathered around any table, engaged in dialogue with friends and family, that time and space is just as sacred, just as infused with the presence of God as any worship service. Attempts to erase the distinction between the normally observed categories of sacred and secular are attempts to claim all of our lives, all of our times, all of our locations as places of worship, places where we live out intimacy with God. This is consistent, is it not, with one of the critical issues we have discussed now in different chapters? We as Christians should, indeed must, increasingly recognize God's call for the complete transformation of all aspects of our lives, from the seemingly mundane to the most elevated. In this sense, attempts at erasing the wall between the sacred and the secular draw attention to the fact that the transforming power of the gospel extends to all aspects of human life.

So, part of the issue with erasing a strong distinction between the sacred and the secular has to do with recognizing the sacredness of all aspects of life. It has to do with reminding us that we, as Christians, are not supposed to come to church on Sunday (or, whatever day your particular congregation meets) to get our weekly "fix" of religion so that we can return to live as secularists the rest of the week. What Deb Hirsch and those like her are trying to do is keep before us the realization that our lives are to be lived constantly in the presence of God, constantly in service and worship to God, constantly aware of the fact that we are to live our lives as representatives of the Sacred everywhere we go.

There is another important, underlying theological point closely related to this whole idea. Perhaps I can clarify the point best by recounting a conversation I once had with a friend. I was telling him about a class I was teaching at the time. A requisite part of this class was to engage in some sort of project that was aimed to serve the reign of God in some way. We called them "kingdom projects." I tended to give students a great deal of leeway on what sorts of projects they might undertake, and I was telling my friend about one that I had found particularly interesting. One student had decided that on every Tuesday night for a six-week period, he would go down to a local bar and stake out a table. He would sit there, drinking soft drinks and engaging with anyone who might be interested in conversation. But, his specific way of being in service to the folks there was that he offered to drive home anyone who had consumed too much alcohol. At the end of the story, my friend made a comment to the effect that he could never do something like that. When I asked why, he responded that he feared being seen in the bar; specifically, he feared that his witness as a Christian would be damaged if someone saw him going into such a place.

I simply listened. Each of us has to make our own judgments about how we respond to God's call of discipleship on our lives. Yet, I have to admit that, while I understood my friend's comments, I could not bring myself to agree with the concern. And, this is where our conversation from this chapter comes to bear: when we as Christians go into a situation like this, we should not be worried that somehow the secularity or even sinfulness of the place will somehow infect the sacredness or holiness we enjoy through God's presence in our lives. No, we should instead see the presence of God we bring to these "secular" places as infecting them with God's presence and holiness.

To put a finer point on it, there were those during the early church period (largely, gnostics) who considered human existence to be corrupt and sinful. They could not imagine God becoming incarnate as human because they could not imagine God being sullied by taking on human flesh. However, the position the church came to embrace affirmed that God did become incarnate in human flesh. In fact, though, the doctrine developed during the early church period largely agreed with the pessimistic view of human sin and corruption. So, why did they not end up agreeing with the gnostics? Because the church did *not* see God's taking on human flesh as somehow sullying God; rather, the church saw things precisely opposite. The belief was that human corruption was *healed* by the divine presence within it. God was not worried that human estrangement would infiltrate the divine holiness; no, instead, God knew that God's holiness would infect and heal that estrangement. We as Christians carry God's Spirit and that divine holiness within us, and we should see ourselves as agents carrying the divine holiness within and serving as agents of healing and reconciliation everywhere we go.[7] Attempts to erase the distinction between the sacred and the secular are partly aimed at reminding us of this fact.

A colleague of mine used to say that the transforming work of the Holy Spirit in our lives had not yet sunk in deeply enough until it impacted how we threw out the trash. Her point was quite simple, I think. She was trying to help folks see that there is no act in which we as Christians might engage that does not represent an opportunity for the full transformative work of God in our lives to shine through. She did so by reminding us that even the most mundane tasks, for example throwing out the trash, are infused with sacred significance if we will but let them be. May we constantly be on the lookout for opportunities to infuse the so-called secular with moments of divine sacredness!

Before I close this chapter, I want to make one additional observation. While I want to argue that churches that are worth getting up for should pay attention to this question of erasing the line between the sacred and the secular, different contexts and different settings are going to require careful attention to determine the best way to take this on. For example, if you are part of a church that has long utilized traditional spaces and formats for worship, you are likely to run into, shall we say, difficulties if you come in next Sunday and suggest you get rid of all the pews. If we alienate a significant portion of our existing congregation, we are probably not moving with adequate care and nuance. In other words, take the Hirsches' example to heart, but apply it in your own setting, in your own way. There are many ways to begin to dismantle an unhealthy distinction between the sacred and the secular, and surely one or more of them will allow you to do that in ways that both respect and challenge the existing congregation.

Chapter 9

Go and Make
Disciples!

*Now the eleven disciples went to Galilee, to the mountain where Jesus told
them to go. When they saw him, they worshipped him, but some doubted.
Jesus came near and spoke to them, "I've received all authority in heaven and
on earth. Therefore, go and make disciples of all nations, baptizing them in the
name of the Father and of the Son and of the Holy Spirit, teaching them to obey
everything that I've commanded you. Look, I myself will be with you every day
until the end of this present age. (Matthew 28:16-20)*

Christians identify this particular passage as the Great Commission.[1]
These words capture the instructions that Jesus gives to his disciples (here,
the eleven, after the death of Judas) regarding the spread of the gospel.
This passage, in many ways, has become the underpinning for much of
the work of the church as the church seeks to be a faithful witness and
spread the gospel. In fact, it is widely accepted that the foundations for
evangelism are to be found in these very words. Given that this passage is
so central to what we as Christians are to do and to be about, it's worth
taking a few moments to attend to the details, in particular, seeing if
there is anything that we might have overlooked in our past readings.[2]

Matthew has several ways of telling us that something he is about
to relate is particularly noteworthy, and one of those ways is to connect

them with the mountain where they occurred. Here, we are told that Jesus had instructed the disciples to meet him at an unnamed mountain. The transfiguration, the temptations, and the Sermon on the Mount are other instances where a mountain location was prominent. Is the idea behind choosing this location the fact that Jesus wants them to be able to survey the world into which he is about to send them?

It is hard not to love the transparency of the Gospels. In this particular case, we are told that when they gathered with Jesus, they worshiped him, but some doubted. It was Paul Tillich who commented that we, as Christians, are always simultaneously in faith and out of faith. Perhaps we are all, to some extent, like the man who responded to Jesus' call for him to have faith by crying out, "I have faith; help my lack of faith!"[3] Why did the disciples doubt or, as Wright suggests, hesitate? Well, we don't know, but it is interesting that Matthew does not try to cover over the realities of the moment in an attempt to make them seem more pious. It's hard not to love that sort of naked transparency.

Have you ever noticed that at this point, post-Resurrection, Jesus claims to have precisely what the devil had offered during the temptations? He had offered Jesus authority over everything if he would but kneel before the devil. Jesus, of course, refused, responding that only God is worthy of such allegiance. Yet, now, as Jesus is at the end of this physical presence on the earth, and as his sacrifice on the cross and his being raised from the dead have been completed, he tells the disciples that all authority has been given to him. There can be no doubt of the implications—through obedience, obedience even to death, as Paul would later put it—Jesus has been exalted by the Father and now has ruling authority over all. So, given that Jesus has been endowed with the authority to rule over the world, the next obvious question is: How is he going to embody that rule? What does his ruling presence look like? And how will that get worked out in the world? Wright's answer to the question is at the same time obvious, humbling, and shocking:

> And how is he going to do this [how is Jesus going to implement his rule characterized by life-giving love]? Here is the shock: *through us,*

his followers. The project only goes forward insofar as Jesus' agents, the people he has commissioned, are taking it forward.[4]

Now, that is worth sitting back and pondering for a moment. The humbling and shocking reality of God's great work of reconciliation of the world is that it has been entrusted to us. In the discussions of previous chapters, we have frequently discussed ways in which the church has failed to embody the life-giving love of its Lord. Yet, Jesus goes directly from affirming his authority to saying, "Therefore, go and make disciples." Whether we like it or not, whether we feel worthy or not, through the Great Commission, Jesus uses the fact that he has been given all authority as the basis for calling upon his disciples to transform the world by extending that rule visibly.

The Great Commission: Making Disciples

Jesus identifies three very closely interrelated activities that instruct us as to how we are to expand the reign of Christ. In fact, the way the text reads, I would suggest that there is one primary thing we are to do, which is supplemented by two other things. The Great Commission primarily enjoins us to *make disciples.* Now, it's worth pausing here for a moment to reflect. What does it mean to say that the primary task given us by the Great Commission is to make *disciples?* First, it is noteworthy that Jesus does not simply say that we should go out and make *converts.* Yet, I find myself wondering if we don't often take it that way. In other words, is it not the case that too often our evangelistic efforts are focused on getting a person to make a profession of faith in Jesus and too little are those efforts focused on bringing about the life of transformation implied by the word "disciple"*?* Before we go on, let's take a look at the two terms and see why we might want to be sympathetic to this distinction.

I believe that the common way in which the term "convert" is understood connects primarily with the changing of a person's beliefs. So, a convert would be a person who *was* committed to some set of beliefs, but through some means of reflection, persuasion, or analysis, has come to be committed to a different set of beliefs. Perhaps I have been a person who has believed, say, that the Austrian school of economics provided the most accurate description of the actual and desired economic outcomes in a society. However, perhaps, upon reading Keynes and studying his critics and supporters, I have come to believe that Keynesianism is superior to the Austrian school. As a result of my study and reflection, I become a *convert* to a different understanding of the economy. My set of beliefs and commitments has changed. To make the example a religious one, imagine a person raised a Buddhist who believed the teachings of Buddhism to be true. Further imagine this person visiting a Christian church with friends and hearing the Christian gospel, perhaps for the first time. Such a person might come to believe the Christian faith to be true and, thus, to *convert* from Buddhism to Christianity. The basic connotation carried by the term "convert" is to identify conversion as the changing of one's beliefs from one belief system to another.

On the other hand, the word "disciple" normally carries with it a deeper meaning, almost certainly a deeper connotation, than just changing one's belief system. The Greek word translated as "disciples" is *mathetes,* and a cursory review of the ways in which the word is used in the New Testament is enlightening.[5] Perhaps the most significant point to note is the deep and personal connection implied by the word, specifically, the personal commitment of the *mathetes* or *disciple* to the person who serves as his or her master/guide/lord.

First, a disciple was not one who simply believed what the master taught, but one who was also personally and intimately connected with the life of the master. The depth of the personal commitment of the disciples to Jesus is surely evident when we read of the fear and chaos they experienced during the period between the Crucifixion and the Resurrection. Jesus was not just a first-century Jew that these other first-century Jews had chosen to pal around with. No, they had so committed themselves to the person of Jesus that his death had left them utterly lost. First and foremost, being a disciple implied a deep personal commitment to the master on the part of the disciple, and to be a disciple of Jesus meant to have that commitment to the person of Jesus.

Second, a disciple was a person who had not only committed him or herself in a deep, personal way to the one deemed master but one who also was obedient to that master. No task was too small or menial as the disciple followed the instruction of the master. Kittel's theological dictionary comments upon the obedience of the first disciples, making the point that this was no normal teacher/student relationship:

> Even more significant is the fact that the disciples unconditionally accepted His authority, not just inwardly by believing in Him, but also outwardly by obeying Him. . . . The picture outlined here finds historical confirmation in two scenes from the last days of Jesus. On the occasion of the entry He sends His disciples to find a donkey (Mk. 11:1ff. par.), and later the disciples at His command make ready the last supper (Mk. 13:12ff. par.). These are services which go far beyond what a תַּלְמִיד־חָכָם was obliged to render his teacher, especially when one considers the detailed conditions under which the disciples fulfilled it. . . .What is to be seen here is more than respect. Jesus is obeyed because it is believed He is the Messiah.[6]

So we see, disciples *were* those who shared the belief of their master, but they were much more than that. They had a deep and intimate personal commitment to their master, and they willingly obeyed his commands. In short, the master had authority over all aspects of their lives, no matter how mundane, no matter how momentous.

Third, a disciple of Jesus was one who was willing, *more* than willing, one who was obligated to suffer along with his or her master. How many times did Jesus warn the disciples of the consequences of following him? Kittel summarizes:

> The nature of the calling of the disciples of Jesus, and their resultant dependence on Him, means that there is nothing in the life of the disciples which is apart from Jesus and His life. With all they have and are they are drawn into fellowship with Him. But, the way of Jesus leads to the cross. Hence, entry into His fellowship as His μαθητής carries with it the obligation to suffer.[7]

While most references in the New Testament that hold out the promise of suffering are applied directly to the twelve, this is not universally the case. There are passages where suffering is held out as the reality for all disciples. So, back to our distinction between *converts* and *disciples*, let us summarize. A *convert* is one who makes a change in his or her beliefs. A convert to Christianity is one who comes to believe the gospel of Jesus is true.[8] It is, first and foremost, a change in the things one *believes.* However, a *disciple* of Jesus is one who does, in fact, believe in the gospel, but the commitment runs much deeper than that. Disciples are deeply and intimately committed to the person of Jesus; disciples are persons who obey the commands Jesus gives, even on the most seemingly insignificant matters; and disciples are persons who understand and expect the reality of suffering alongside and on behalf of Jesus.

It is because we often make the bar too low for the task identified by the Great Commission that we have taken the time to dig into these details. Churches that are worth getting up for are the ones that have rightly understood and effectively communicate the obligations and expectations that go along with being a disciple of Jesus. Before we move beyond the use of the term "disciple," there is one more point to be examined.

In these four verses, it is significant to note the appearance of the term "disciple" twice. The first refers to the eleven who followed Jesus, the twelve minus Judas. We are told that the eleven had gathered as Jesus had instructed, but that some "doubted." Earlier I indicated that the reasons for this were unclear, but perhaps we can speculate a possible scenario. Recall that in Matthew we move directly from the resurrection narrative to this appearance to the eleven on the mountain. For Matthew's Gospel, this is the first time the disciples had seen Jesus since his death. Peter had denied Jesus, and the disciples had become deeply distraught over his death, sure that the movement Jesus had birthed was dead with him. Perhaps the "doubt," or perhaps even better, the "hesitation" as Wright suggests, was there because the personal commitment had been broken and needed restoration.[9] Jesus has called them to himself, personally, to assure them of his resurrection and to make clear to them that whatever fears, doubts, or betrayals of which they might be guilty, all is forgiven and right relationship is restored. He has called them together both to assure them of his love for them, regardless of what might have happened in the last few days, as well as to instruct them on their mission going forward.

What seems even more significant, though, is that Matthew records Jesus using the very same word when he commissions the eleven. They are to make disciples—that is, *they are to replicate themselves.* Their task is not just to persuade folks to change belief systems, to persuade them to embrace the ideas that Jesus taught. No, their task is to make disciples, to offer the gospel to others with the goal of making them disciples of Jesus in every sense as fully as the eleven are. Their task will not be complete until they have encouraged persons into deep and intimate relationships with the living Jesus. The Great Commission will not be accomplished unless they help individuals understand the obedience required of one who chooses to become a disciple of Jesus. Finally, the spread of the gospel must carry with it the brutal and honest recognition that following Jesus is expected to lead to suffering for the disciple. It will not always do so—lead to suffering—but suffering ought always to be *expected* as part of what it means to be a disciple of Jesus.

Make Disciples, Baptize, Teach Obedience

Above, I indicated that there were three things Jesus names in this passage as part of the Great Commission. The central point is to *make disciples.* The other two points support the goal of making disciples. Right after his instruction to make disciples, Jesus tells his followers to *baptize* disciples in the name of the Triune God—in the name of the Father, the Son, and the Holy Spirit. The sacrament of baptism is the ritual that marks the official entry into the life of the church. It marks us, to use Scripture's image, as ones sealed by the Holy Spirit, as the ones who have changed allegiance, now commending themselves wholly to God. As a popular ritual reads, baptism is an outward and visible sign of an inner grace. Baptism is a work of God, but it is undertaken publicly so that the one baptized might make an open and visible statement of commitment to the gospel of Christ.

Immediately after instructing that those being made disciples are to be baptized, Jesus tells the eleven that they are to teach them "to obey everything that I've commanded you." As we've noted already, the term "disciple" carries with it the idea of obedience to the master. Here, Jesus makes it explicit—he has taught the eleven what they are supposed to do, how they are to "be" in the world. Because he has given them his commandments, he can tell them to pass his commandments on to those whom they are fashioning into the next disciples. With what do those commandments deal? As we discussed in the last chapter, pretty much everything about how we live our day-to-day lives.

In the course of my interviews, the theme of discipleship was evident throughout. Let me use just one example. In talking with Mike Slaughter, he made a comment that all of us engaged in church renewal should consider:

> As I was growing as a young minister, the attention was always on numbers, how to get more folks into the pews of your church. I studied everything I could get my hands on that would help me understand how better to attract people to church. At Ginghamsburg, we got pretty good at it. Over time, though, my focus has become more and more on making disciples, helping folks to understand and then to respond fully to the transforming power of the Holy Spirit. Having thousands show up on a weekend for church is a humbling and powerful experience. But, as Jesus made clear, it only takes a handful of fully committed disciples to change the world![10]

Others interviewed used different images, but the point was the same: churches that are worth getting up for, churches that make a difference, are the ones that take discipleship seriously.

Many contemporary churches have taken the approach that the bar to becoming disciples should be kept low to make church membership and participation more attractive. Perhaps some think that the barriers to entry should be kept low, and then later offer discipleship training as a supplement to church participation. Is that working, though? Is it the case that by keeping expectations low, we will meet with more numerical success? Well, in the first place, as Slaughter notes above, focusing purely on numerical success overlooks too much. In particular, it overlooks the amazing results God can achieve with a smaller number of fully committed disciples. Secondly, there is little evidence to suggest that reduced expectations result in greater numerical success. In fact, there is a lot of evidence that suggests that churches that have higher expectations actually have better results—both numerically and missionally.

A common finding about the under-30 demographic is the sentiment that they want to change the world. World changing is not easy, but history shows that a small number of sold-out disciples of Jesus can do just that. If we want to be churches that are worth getting up for, let's give our congregations a vision for what God can do through them when they become serious disciples. Then, let's call them to that, and do all we can to empower them to become the best disciples the world has ever seen.

Chapter 10

Using All the Tools

Technological developments of the last thirty years have opened the door to doing ministry in ways never before thought possible. We have smart phones that have more capacity than the average desktop computer did twenty years ago, and laptop computers that can out-perform machines that once took a large room to house. Audiovisual equipment is becoming increasingly sophisticated and functional while becoming less expensive. The Internet makes research and data sharing easier than ever before. In fact, many churches are inexpensively hosting their weekly sermons on their own server, broadcasting their messages out over the Internet. If your church is too small to afford its own servers, though, services such as iTunes and YouTube make it very cost effective to share weekly services.[1]

For example, Olu Brown, lead pastor at Impact Church in Atlanta, told me that they stream their Sunday morning service in order to allow folks literally around the globe to participate in real time with those located on their physical campus. Brown told me that he keeps track of his virtual attenders, who now run into the hundreds. Getting the message of the gospel out to the world from this standpoint has never been easier.

As with all paradigm-shifting technological developments, there are both those who praise the potential it brings as well as those who worry about negative consequences. For example, I've heard folks say, "Yes, but those relationships that persons develop on the Internet are not *real* relationships. You have to be face-to-face for that." Well, while it is true that the Internet enables *different* kinds of relationships, it seems going too far to suggest that they are not real relationships at all. Some may put the question this way: Can the work of the church really be carried out effectively over media like the Internet? I would suggest that the more relevant question is a different one: How can we take advantage of this amazing plethora of tools now available to us in ways that let us effectively carry out the work to which God has called the church? In other words, the focus should not be on *whether* this can be done but rather be upon *how.*

Consider some of the perhaps startling statistics. If you look at the total number of Internet users around the world, estimates put that at 2.4 billion or about one in every three persons globally. That would mean that a ministry of the gospel with an Internet account has the potential to reach one-third of the world's population. It is estimated that there are a billion Internet users in Asia, half a billion in Europe, about a quarter of a billion in North America and Latin America, and then just under 200 million in Africa. Facebook, the world's largest social media network, now boasts over a billion users worldwide. Let that sink in—one out of every seven persons on the planet has an account on and is accessible via Facebook. Granted, that number is disputed, but let's say it's off by half. That still represents access to a pretty amazing number of people. Twitter, the social media network that allows one to share short, 140-character messages, claims to have one half billion users worldwide. LinkedIn, a business and profession-oriented social media network, has 160,000,000 users.[2] Is it any wonder that many church websites have strategically located the little symbols that allow visitors to link immediately through one or more social media sites?

Churches worth getting up for are increasingly the churches where leadership has been aggressive in identifying new technologies and has been equally aggressive in figuring out how to effectively use these new, innovative tools. For example, usage of these technologies increases as you go down in age demographic, which suggests that successfully using these technologies becomes more important as your target church crowd is younger. So, as with other aspects of our work, context and need vary from one church to another. However, we would be remiss not to take at least one chapter to focus on how these different tools are being used by churches today.

The different ways in which technological developments (including the extent to which technology has become more affordable) are being utilized varies widely. That, coupled with the rapid pace of change, makes it futile to attempt even an overview of the different uses. So, the approach I will use in this chapter will be to identify some over-arching categories for the utilization of technology in churches and a number of links that will let the reader experience how some churches and church leaders are using the available tools.

Sermon Preparation

As I'm sure most—if not all—of you know, with relatively minimal investment, in fact with as little as a computer and an Internet con-nection, pastors and teachers within the church will find an incredible array of tools at their fingertips. Let's consider preaching. There are numerous computer-based software packages that can serve a preacher in the task of sermon preparation. In addition, thousands of websites can provide support. Let's say you are planning to preach on a particu-lar passage of Scripture, but you want to see how a number of different translations treat the passage. Various websites as well as a variety of software packages will allow you to lay them all out side by side on your screen. Let's say it's a New Testament passage and you want to see the original Greek. Again, as close as your fingertips. If there is a key word in the passage, and you want to see how often it appears in the New Testament (or in the Bible as a whole), search features that allow you to find out are central parts of many Bible tools. You want sermon illustrations? Again, as close as a fingertip.

I have often been amazed at how little contemporary Christians are aware of the positions the early church took on the various passages from which we compose our sermons. For example, a quick Google search for Luke 12 and Augustine will immediately identify a seemingly endless number of passages that can be studied and utilized. Now, one has to readily admit that what you will find from a search like this is going to be a mixed bag. Some results will be very good, some results will be very bad, and there will be a bunch in between. Consultation with others, attention to the source of the content, and appropriate caution will provide the guidance needed to determine which sources are dependable. Beyond seeing how the early church fathers might have understood a particular passage, you can read numerous sermons from other preachers from throughout the history of the church. Do you want to know how John Wesley dealt with the Sermon on the Mount? Easily found! Do you wonder how your sisters and brothers in another denomination are preaching on a particular passage? Again, one of the many available search engines will let you quickly locate exemplars.

The tools available to preachers today, though, are not just content oriented. If you want to improve your delivery, you can find endless sermons online by popping over to YouTube. Want to hear Otis Moss III preach on the thugs of the Old Testament? Gregg Boyd preach on nationalism? Nadia Bolz-Weber preach to the Lutheran youth assembly? Chances are, if you have a favorite preacher, you can find a sermon by them somewhere online. You can study the styles of different preachers and use that study to help hone your own style. Then, if you like, you can record yourself, upload it to YouTube (or another video sharing site), and invite comments on content and style. The opportunities are endless.

One last point on sermon preparation. Whatever one thinks of Hollywood, they are experts at making a point, and the careful integration of a poignant clip can help you get your point across. When I teach seminary classes, I frequently use audio or video clips as teaching tools. I fear that some see utilizing such clips as lazy, an easy way out of serious sermon preparation, but my experience is quite the opposite. The effective deployment of a well-chosen audio or video clip is hardly lazy, given the thought and care it takes to make sure it is well integrated into the flow of the sermon. In addition, I have often been amazed at how deeply a well-done audio or video clip can move a congregation to grasp important points. Let me say it again: preachers today have an unprecedented array of tools to help them be the most effective communicators of the good news, and we should be taking advantage of every one of them!

Using Technology for Church

I want to give one more example of ways that churches can use the technology available to them to proclaim the gospel, and then I will take the remainder of the chapter to provide links that exemplify some of the things we have discussed. A few hours looking at how others are successfully deploying these tools will provide more guidance than a lengthy discourse.

For a few years, I was living in a place where my friends and I were having a hard time locating a church within our tradition that consistently emphasized the points we thought critical to the gospel. However, I knew of another church, in another location, that was. Now, this particular church posted the sermon from that week by Monday or Tuesday of the following week, that is, within a day or two of its original delivery. The frustration level with my friends and me got to the point that we considered renting a space on Sunday morning and constructing a worship service around the video of the preacher's sermon from the previous week. Our plan was, essentially, to follow a normal order of worship, including serving Communion, and concluding with discussion around the sermon topic. In fact, the church we were planning to follow had considered developing downloadable resources that would help empower folks like us. Is it ideal? I suppose that's debatable, but it was one solution to a very real problem.

I suggest we not be surprised if this model grows over the next few years, allowing groups to gather under the lordship of Christ, in essence, a remote embodiment of the other church. If we look at economic trends, one can find a number of reasons why a model that allows small, dispersed house churches essentially to partner with bigger, better resourced churches seems a likely direction for the future of the church. There is widespread agreement that there will need to be a major rethink of what it means to be and do church. I suggest the increasing use of technology will be one of the consequences of rethinking church. In other words, churches that are worth getting up for will not be reticent to take full advantage of all the tools available.

Some Examples

In the following paragraphs, I list several examples of how web-based technology and social media tools are being used today, mostly by church leaders whom I interviewed for this project.

Below are links to the Facebook pages of most of the interviewees. Take a little bit of time to explore each one, noting how they are using the medium to be able to connect with Christians engaged with their ministry. Many of these folks are utilizing programs that allow them to seamlessly integrate the content they provide on a variety of platforms. For example, when Brian McLaren posts something on his website, the first part of the post is "tweeted" immediately to his Twitter account. It also appears on his Facebook page without any further effort on his part.

Facebook

Nadia Bolz-Weber: facebook.com/sarcasticlutheran

Greg Boyd: facebook.com/gregoryaboyd

Alan Hirsch: facebook.com/alanhirsch

Brian McLaren: facebook.com/pages/Brian-D-McLaren /65814657989?fref=ts

Ros Picardo: facebook.com/pastorrosariopicardo

Mike Slaughter: facebook.com/michael.slaughter 2?fref=ts

Many pastors/church leaders operate their own unique websites. These provide the opportunity to post longer content and video or audio content or even conduct surveys within a context that allows the reader to focus. As noted, the content is often automatically posted on their Facebook pages as well. However, a dedicated website allows readers to interact with the content provided without being distracted by the constantly updated feeds that generally comprise the Facebook experience. One need not pick one outlet or the other—just link them and use them both, allowing readers to access content in the way that best suits them.

Individual Websites

Nadia Bolz-Weber: sarcasticlutheran.com

Greg Boyd: reknew.org

Al Hirsch: theforgottenways.org

Brian McLaren: brianmclaren.net

Rosario Picardo: rosariopicardo.com

Chris Seay: chrisseay.net

Mike Slaughter: mikeslaughter.com

While leaders often have their own websites, it seems that most churches have established a presence on Facebook. You may or may not decide to use an individual page on Facebook or a personal website, but here are some fine examples of how churches are using the media.

Churches Using Facebook

Ecclesia: facebook.com/ecclesiahouston

Embrace Church: facebook.com/embraceyourcity.com

House for All Sinners and Saint: facebook.com/Houseforall

Ginghamsburg UMC: facebook.com/Ginghamsburg

Impact Church: facebook.com/impactdoingchurchdifferently

Woodland Hills: facebook.com/woodlandhillschurch

Church Website

Ecclesia: ecclesiahouston.org

Embrace: embraceyourcity.com

House for All Sinners and Saints: houseforall.org

Ginghamsburg UMC: ginghamsburg.org

Impact Church: impactdoingchurchdifferently.org

Tribe: tribela.com

Woodland Hills: whchurch.org

YouTube

YouTube, as mentioned earlier, allows users to upload video content to the web. The potential uses are endless—wider distribution of sermons, teaching on particular doctrine or practices, music performances, and on and on. I've provided links to sample sermons or other video content from a number of the folks interviewed for this project and from other pastors whose work I know. I'd encourage you to sample several of them. In some cases, the equipment used is quite sophisticated, but in others, much less so. It can be done on virtually any size budget.

Nadia Bolz-Weber: youtube.com/watch?v=kM9Y5S3UYi8

Greg Boyd: youtube.com/watch?v=Sw5GLq5O
-50&feature=share

Freddie Haynes: youtube.com/watch?v=WDacTmH8PwU

Alan Hirsch: youtube.com/watch?v=mwBEWNn4FTw

Brian McLaren: youtube.com/watch?v=H2g8Iz5riVs

Otis Moss III: youtube.com/watch?v=RO0WrF-t95A

Ros Picardo: youtube.com/watch?v=9H-Z-CUZ6oM

Chris Seay: youtube.com/watch?v=spCgZeLXmWU

Mike Slaughter: youtube.com/ginghamsburg.org/sermons
/resources/952

It's a great time to be alive, to be a participant in God's great work of reconciliation of the world. Never has there been a time when there have been more ways to get the message out. You don't have to use them all, by any means, but let me encourage you to take some time to explore and to determine which might best serve the context you are in. Just keep in mind: using the tools we have discussed in this chapter is not cheating, it's not taking shortcuts, nor is it capitulating to the spirit of the technological age in which we live. No, if anything it is more the equivalent of "plundering the Egyptians." So, let's take advantage of all the tools as we seek to be faithful to spreading the good news around the block and around the world!

Chapter 11

Moving Forward with Hope

One look at the worsening demographic trends vis-à-vis the church and it's easy to become quite discouraged. The negative impression of the church held by the very people we, as the church, want to successfully engage can result in dismay. The sheer magnitude of the work that we need to do on ourselves is nothing short of overwhelming. So, if the reader is feeling a little depressed and discouraged at this point, well, that would be understandable.

Yet, dismay and discouragement are not the last word. The reasons to be hopeful are numerous, as are the reasons to be optimistic that churches can once again be seen as places worth getting up for. I see seven reasons that the future of the church is filled with hope, in spite of the bad news. Let's consider some of those seeds of hope in the proverbial mountain of problems.

Seven Reasons to Be Filled with Hope

1. Scripture teaches us that hope is never in vain when it is centered in a God who cannot fail.

2. There is now and forever will be hope in the life, death, and resurrection of Jesus.

3. The Holy Spirit is still in the transforming and sanctifying business.

4. As we become more and more willing to own our shortcomings, we become more and more open to God's transforming power.

5. Many churches are turning attention to missional concerns and are asking more penetrating questions about what it means to be in mission to the world.

6. There is hope in a new generation that has a heart and a desire to "change the world."

7. A sense that old paradigms no longer work is prevalent and a willingness to challenge and change those old paradigms is increasingly evident.

So, let's look at each of these seven more in depth:

1. Scripture teaches us that hope is never in vain when it is centered in a God who cannot fail. During the course of his ministry on earth, Jesus surrounded himself with a dozen disciples. Think about that for a minute, just 12, and as we all know, one of them turned out to be a betrayer. Now, it's not simply that Jesus surrounded himself with only a dozen disciples, but look at those he picked. I mean, this was a rag-tag team if there ever was one—fishermen, tax collectors, a political zealot (talk about partisan politics!), and so it goes. Don't misunderstand me, I am not demeaning the vocations of the disciples. But let's face it, if you were putting together a group that you wanted to help you turn the world upside down, this is not exactly the group that you would likely choose for your A team. No, for this job, you want skilled politicians, perhaps military leaders, certainly folks well-heeled and ready, willing, and able to fund the work. Yet, there it is, plain as the nose on your face. Jesus, charged with turning the world on its head, picks this crew as his first string. Well, you know what? If Jesus, way back in the first century, could pick this rag-tag team of a mere dozen for his world-jarring enterprise, well, maybe, just maybe, he can do it again . . . with us.

The Lord we serve, the Holy Spirit that empowers us, the God and Father of us all who sends them and us into the world, this triune God simply does not know how to fail. The first reason we Christians have to be hopeful is that God is still in the business of turning the world upside down. The job is not a cushy one. Remember, the lives of the first dozen pretty much ended violently, in service to their Lord. But, what God can do with followers who are all-in is nothing short of amazing—and profoundly hopeful.

2. There is now and forever will be hope in the life, death, and resurrection of Jesus. The apostle Paul writes that if Christ be not raised from the dead, then we Christians, of all people, are the most to be pitied. For Paul, the reality of the resurrection is the very centerpiece of the good news. No resurrection; no good news. Throughout Scripture, there are places where God brings life from what seems to be certain death or despair. Abraham and Sarah had given up hope of having a child of their own, but God breathed new life into what seemed barren. The plight of the oppressed Israelites seemed hopeless in Egypt, yet God raised Moses to take a message of new life to them. Elizabeth and Zechariah become late in life the parents of John the Baptist. God seems to be in the "snatching-victory-from-the-jaws-of-defeat" business, and the Resurrection is the prime example of that. The disciples had given up after seeing Jesus die on the cross. They were heartbroken, no doubt sure their hope and trust had been incorrectly placed in Jesus. But, then God would vindicate their faith when Jesus was raised from the dead.

While the church looks dead in many places around the world, in many places resurrection is breaking out, new life is being breathed into the old bones. Just as the Spirit raised Jesus from the dead, so can the Spirit reawaken a seemingly dead church to new life. The power of the Resurrection provides hope for us in the church today, hope that reminds us we need not despair but rather work to realign ourselves with the wonder-working power of God, the power that can (and will, if we but let it) give new life to the church.

3. The Holy Spirit is still in the transforming and sanctifying business. That we can be transformed and empowered by the Holy Spirit to live the life that pleases God is a common theme throughout Scripture. In the Old Testament, for example, the prophet Joel connects the outpouring of God's Spirit with empowerment to carry out God's work.

Later, in Acts, Peter would connect this very passage with the ministry of the church. We are told that Jesus is empowered by the Spirit, and after his death on the cross, it is the Spirit that raises him from the dead. In Luke, we read that it is the Spirit that drives Jesus out into the desert for his time of testing. Then, immediately after, he returns to Galilee and begins to preach in the synagogues. In verse 18 of Luke 4, Jesus begins the reading from the prophet Isaiah by saying that "The Spirit of the Lord is upon me." When we identify reasons to be hopeful, in spite of the negative indicators, surely our ongoing faith in the power of the Holy Spirit to bring new life sits at the center of that hope.

Within the Wesleyan tradition, we are heirs to John Wesley's doctrine of sanctification. The primary point of the doctrine is to make clear the empowering work of the Holy Spirit. In short, the doctrine of sanctification reminds us that God does not call us to undertake a task unless God is ready and willing to empower us to accomplish it. We need not go into too much detail, but a quick summary of Wesley's order of salvation is helpful at this point. Wesley saw God's grace working with us, throughout this life, in distinct ways that had particular outcomes in mind. He spoke of prevenient grace, convicting grace, justifying grace, and sanctifying grace.

- All humans are recipients of prevenient grace, according to Wesley, and this grace frees us from the worst effects of our sin so that we might respond to God.

- Prevenient grace is the phrase Wesley used to describe the Spirit's interaction with humans; it makes us aware of our need for forgiveness and healing.

- Justifying grace is that grace of God that begins the work of transformation. Our relationship with God is restored when we are justified and we begin to follow Jesus.

- Sanctifying grace is what empowers persons, as Wesley would say, to love God with their whole hearts and to love their neighbors as themselves. It is the realization of God's life-transforming work in us.

Interestingly, Wesley often used the metaphor of a house to further illumine these different graces—prevenient grace is the porch of salvation, he would say. For him, justifying grace is only the door to salvation, because it is only the beginning of God's transforming work. It is at the act of sanctification that we begin to live in the house, to continue Wesley's metaphor. When our desire to follow and obey God becomes deepest, we open ourselves to the presence of the Spirit in such a way that the Spirit's transforming power becomes fully operational. We are empowered to love God with our whole heart and to love our neighbors as ourselves. That empowerment spills over into all that we do, including how we function as the church. The transforming power of the Holy Spirit gives us hope that the church can be healed and restored to the place God intends for it.

4. *As we become more and more willing to own our shortcomings, we become more and more open to God's transforming power.* There can be no real change in the ways in which we interact with each other until we realize that our current approach is a problem. Once we are open to admitting our failures, then the possibility of transformation becomes a real option for us. This is where the studies like those embodied in the book *unChristian* can be so helpful to us. They set before us popular perceptions of how we as Christians behave, and they encourage us to correct our bad behaviors. Scripture reveals to us again and again the picture of a God always ready to forgive, always ready to empower us to change, if we will realize our flaws and repent of them. In fact, it is often the case that the biggest obstacle to change in our life is spiritual pride, the unwillingness to admit our mistakes, attempting instead to transfer the blame somewhere else.

Consider the story Jesus tells in Luke 18:9-14, the story commonly known as the parable of the publican and the sinner.

> Jesus told this parable to certain people who had convinced themselves that they were righteous and who looked on everyone else with disgust. "Two people went up to the temple to pray. One was a Pharisee and the other a tax collector. The Pharisee stood and prayed about himself with these words, 'God, I thank you that I'm not like

119

everyone else—crooks, evildoers, adulterers—or even like this tax collector. I fast twice a week. I give a tenth of everything I receive.' But the tax collector stood at a distance. He wouldn't even lift his eyes to look toward heaven. Rather, he struck his chest and said, 'God, show mercy to me, a sinner.' I tell you, this person went down to his home justified rather than the Pharisee. All who lift themselves up will be brought low, and those who make themselves low will be lifted up."

It is easy for us to rationalize our own behaviors, focusing on the places where we do well. Here, the Pharisee compares himself to the tax collector, a person despised by the first-century Jewish community. He racks up quite an impressive comparison, sure that God is far more pleased with him than with the tax collector. Yet, the twist in the story comes when Jesus declares that the one who recognizes and owns his sins, who beats his chest with despair begging God for mercy, is the one who will be lifted up. When we humble ourselves, looking for mercy, wanting to be transformed, these are the times when God is most able to work change within us.

As we noted in chapter 3, many have responded to the criticisms embodied in analyses like *unChristian* in much the same manner as the Pharisee in this parable. We are sure we are doing things well; we are sure that the criticisms offered by the culture are more a sign of their perversity than ours. While many have responded defensively, not all have. I think the fact that many are hearing and repenting of those behaviors is another basis for hope—hope that when we face our sin, God will help us to overcome it.

5. Many churches are turning attention to missional concerns and are asking more penetrating questions about what it means to be in mission to the world. This not only means our willingness to get outside ourselves but also concerns deepening discipleship, which is our willingness to be inwardly transformed. I must say that one of the most significant reasons for hope that has come along in the last 50 years has been the increasing attention to matters related to mission. In particular, the "missional movement" gives me great cause for hope. For much of the modern period, our approach to church has been conducted along what has commonly been called the "attractional model," creating churches that are effective at attracting folks to our services. We want our facilities to be top-of-the-line; we script our services very carefully. However, while there are places where the attractional model prevails, it seems increasingly to be giving way to a more missions-oriented model—a model that focuses on we Christians going out, rather than our only trying to draw others in.

I should be careful to note that to affirm the missional model of church is not to suggest that gathering together for worship is to be avoided or ignored. Gathering together for corporate worship will almost certainly continue to be an important part of churches that are worth getting up for.

The reason I find such hope in the missional movement is that it reminds us of who we as the church are supposed to be and what we are supposed to be about. As the old saying goes, the church is the one organization in the world that exists primarily to be in service to those around them. In other words, we primarily exist not for ourselves but for others. Again and again, the biblical narratives call us to put the interests of the "other" above our own. When we really let this sink in, then our focus becomes much more missional, much more aligned with the idea of existing for the sake of the world. As we engage in mission, we imitate the God who best models what it means to be in mission through the Incarnation. As I said, this missional focus is a tremendous source of hope.

6. There is hope in a new generation that has a heart and a desire to "change the world." Demographic studies that look at the group that is roughly 35 and under often characterize them as a generation that wants to change the world. They are much less interested in the abstract and much more interested in the concrete—how does the life of faith get worked out in our interactions with each other? What are we supposed to be doing? It's not that the more abstract components of the faith are unimportant. Rather, I would say that the next generation appears to have a much healthier balance between the two.

Jim Wallis, founder of the social justice ministry Sojourners, tells the following story about one of his speaking events. After the presentation, he was signing books and visiting with the folks who had been in attendance. A young girl (he would later find out she was only eight) came up and started talking to him. She was deeply concerned about the different challenges that Wallis had talked about during the presentation, and she was clearly sympathetic to the perspective he had. So, at one point, he asked her, "Well, what do you think we need to do about those problems?" To which she responded, hands on hips, "Well, Mr. Wallis, I guess we are just going to have to change the world!" There, in a nutshell, is the spirit that we find in many of the next generation—a can-do attitude if there ever was one. When I consider the reasons why we should be hopeful that the church can be restored, that it can again become relevant and a strong force for transformation in our culture, the spirit of that particular demographic is right at the top.

7. A sense that old paradigms no longer work is prevalent and a willingness to challenge and change those old paradigms is increasingly evident. I could have incorporated this into the last point, but it seemed worth mentioning separately. Not only is the next generation one that has the energy and spirit to change the world, but the members are also, as most next generations are, quite willing to rethink traditions. They do not have the emotional attachments that many of us have to doing church "the way we always have." We will need to experiment with new paradigms, find out what is effective and what is not, and then make long-term decisions about how to structure churches that will be worth getting up for. I am hopeful at the entrepreneurial, think-outside-the-box attitude that so many of the younger church leaders have. May we older leaders be careful to mentor them in ways that release rather than disempower their creative spirits.

Preach, Teach, and Live Out the Message of Hope

I conclude our study together of what will help to build churches that are worth getting up for by reminding us all of something we already know: churches worth getting up for are churches that know how to preach hope to their congregations. It is not enough to have hope, however. We have to learn how to effectively communicate hope through the sermons we preach regularly. As we noted at the outset, demographic trends are not encouraging. And, if those trends continue as they are unfolding currently, then the future of the church in the West is discouraging indeed. However, part of creating hope, part of realizing hope is wrapped up with preaching hope. When our congregations come to hear us, they need to hear the challenges, they need to hear the future to which God is calling us, and, of course, they need to hear about our need to repent. But, if our sermons stay focused at the level of critique, we will eventually cause our congregations to become disillusioned and without hope. There is nothing more dangerous to the life of the church than the loss of hope. We need to adjust our sermons in ways that both challenge and give hope, that both identify our weaknesses and call us to the better angels of our natures.

As noted above, we have many reasons to be hopeful about the future of the church even in light of the challenges we face. Take those reasons for hope and use them as words of encouragement to your congregations. Remind them to take hope in the God of hope. When they do, the God of hope will renew our energy, and we will grow more and more to be the people God created us to be. Take hope, and let's change the world!

NOTES

Introduction

1. Interestingly, one wonders the extent to which Luke's Gospel makes the same point when he has the first demon exorcism occurring within the synagogue. Luke seemed to be reminding us that we too often overlook the "demons at home" in order to present ourselves as more on the ball than we are.

2. See my *The Right Church: Living Like the First Christians* (Nashville: Abingdon, 2012) for a more detailed discussion on the different ways in which the term "freedom" is used in our culture. There I argue that we over-emphasize the "freedom to do as we please," and under-emphasize the much more biblical idea of freedom as freedom from sin.

3. Remembering, of course, that the Great Commission sends us out to make disciples, not just converts.

Chapter 1: Putting Jesus Back at the Center

1. We could similarly name products that have bad brand associations—brands that bring bad experiences and expectations to mind. I'll leave that, though, as an exercise for the reader.

2. Chapter 3.

3. I realize I am combining the term "Christian" with the term "church" here. While a more nuanced discussion would require more careful distinction, I think this level of detail is adequate for this chapter's points.

4. David Kinnaman and Gabe Lyons, *unChristian: What a New Generation Really Thinks about Christianity . . . and Why It Matters* (Grand Rapids: Baker Books, reprint edition, 2012).

5. I am indebted to Alan Hirsch for this particular example.

6. Whether Ghandi actually said it matters little. It captures a common sentiment regardless.

7. Speaking of the doctrinal affirmations the church developed is intended in no way to undermine the authority or correctness of those affirmations as embodied in the early church creeds.

8. As evidenced by numerous studies. For example, several over the years by the Barna Group.

9. Here we focus on the life of Jesus in particular. In chapter 3, we will look at several issues in more detail.

10. Alan Hirsch, interview by author, April 2012.

11. N. T. Wright, *The Challenge of Jesus* (IVP, 2009).

12. Chris Seay, interview by author, April 2012.

13. Mark 10:29-30.

Chapter 2: The Value of Authenticity

1. I'll say more in a moment, but don't read the desire to be loved as we really are to imply that we have no desire to change or to overcome our faults.

2. Annie Dillard, *Teaching a Stone to Talk* (Harper and Row, 1982), p. 40.

3. http://www.boston.com/bostonglobe/ideas/articles/2010/07/11/how_facts _backfire/.

Chapter 3: The Big Six

1. David Kinnaman and Gabe Lyons, *unChristian: What a New Generation Really Thinks about Christianity . . . and Why It Matters* (Grand Rapids: Baker, 2007).

2. Ibid., 11.

3. Ibid., 29–30.

4. Ibid., 18.

5. Cited by Christine Walker in *The Dallas Morning News*. http://www
.adherents.com/largecom/baptist_divorce.html.

6. Ibid.

7. Kinnaman and Lyons, *unChristian*, 69.

8. In fact, the altar call is a rather late invention within church history, probably dating back only a little more than 200 years, and then, primarily within
certain strands of Protestantism.

9. I've gone into this in more detail in *Christians and the Common Good*
(Grand Rapids: Brazos, 2011).

10. Mike Slaughter and Charles E. Gutenson, *Hijacked: Responding to the
Partisan Church Divide* (Nashville: Abingdon, 2012).

11. Which is not to say that there is anything wrong with an individual's
decision not to participate. The concern is when an individual's decision not to
participate becomes a normative claim about participating.

Chapter 4: Radical Hospitality

1. Nadia Bolz-Weber, interview by author, April 2012.

2. Revelation 7:9.

3. In due course, we'll have to consider just how hospitable we really are if we
sit back and wait for people to find us rather than actively engaging in reaching
out to them.

4. Father Daniel Homan and Lonni Collins Pratt, *Radical Hospitality:
Benedict's Way of Love* (Brewster, MA: Paraclete Press, 2005), 2–5.

5. James 2:15-17.

6. Philip Yancey, *What's So Amazing about Grace?* (Grand Rapids: Zondervan,
1997), 131.

7. Luke 14:12-14.

8. I am using the phrase "things we consider to be sins" because the point here has nothing to do with who is right or wrong about which activities are sins and which ones are not. The issue is one of hospitality, not of the judgments of individual acts.

Chapter 5: Rebalancing

1. I want to be clear that in focusing on these roles, I intend no loss of focus on the critical role the Holy Spirit plays in renewal and revival of the church. The issue here is trying to make sure we fulfill the roles and responsibilities that God intends *for us* as well.

2. Ephesians 4:11-13.

3. Find the article "Three Over-looked Leadership Roles," in *Leadership Journal*, Spring 2008, at: http://www.christianitytoday.com/le/2008/spring/7.32.html.

4. Ibid. As with all things, some nuance is always helpful. I take his comment that "our seminaries were not producing them" to be a judgment about the relative outcomes he was seeing. There were many more teachers and pastors being produced than apostles, evangelists, and prophets.

5. It would be interesting to explore the terms translated as "measure" and "full stature" to get an even richer sense of what Paul has in mind, but that extends beyond our purpose here.

6. "APEST Descriptions," Alan Hirsch, 2009, www.theforgottenways.org.

7. See Al Hirsch's latest work, coauthored with Tim Catchim, *The Permanent Revolution: Apostolic Imagination and Practice for the Twenty-first Century Church* (San Francisco: Jossey-Bass, 2012) for more details and defense for the five-fold ministry described in chapter 4.

8. Christopher J. H. Wright, *The Mission of the People of God: A Biblical Theology of the Church's Mission* (Grand Rapids: Zondervan, 2010).

9. See my *The Right Church: Live Like the First Christians* (Nashville: Abingdon, 2012) for more detail.

Chapter 6: Focus, Focus, Focus

1. Given our focus, in what follows, we will give attention on the Lord's Supper.

2. We have transliterated a word from Greek to English if we have used the letters in English closest to those in Greek. So, for example, an alpha in Greek becomes an *a* in English; a beta in Greek becomes a *b* in English, and so on.

3. *Theological Dictionary of the New Testament*, vol. II, ed. Gerhard Kittel and Gerhard Friedrich, trans. G. W. Bromiley (Grand Rapids: Eerdmans, 1964), p. 731.

4. Though, we must not overlook the concrete "this worldly" aspect of forgiveness, because the healing of many broken relationships between humans is also a place where seeking and giving forgiveness for the ways in which we hurt each other is critical.

5. And, of course, we often include "Holy" in the description of these celebrations.

6. Consider, for example, the English word "prognosis," which has its root in two Greek terms: a prefix *pro* and a stem *gnosis*. However, the English word "proper" does not break down in the same way. This is just a reminder that words do not always divide up in neat and predictable ways.

Chapter 7: Right Belief, Right Practice: Equal Partners?

1. A similar breakdown in agreement can happen around the pair orthopraxy and evangelism. Is the church's main task to live out the gospel in certain ways? Or is it primarily to testify to the newness of life made possible by the sacrifice of Christ? We will bounce back and forth somewhat between the points, but recognize that the underlying disagreements are quite similar.

2. And, of course, once you say that right belief is "all that the Bible teaches," the next debate will be about the differing views as to what Scripture teaches. Thankfully, this is not a debate we have to get into here to address our overarching concerns.

3. James 2:19-20: "It's good that you believe that God is one. Ha! Even the demons believe this, and they tremble with fear. Are you so slow? Do you need to be shown that faith without actions has no value at all?"

4. Ronald J. Sider, Philip N. Olson, Heidi Unruh, *Churches That Make a Difference: Reaching Your Community with Good News and Good Works* (Baker: Grand Rapids, 2002), 13.

5. This sermon series has since been the subject of a book (aptly entitled *Christmas Is Not Your Birthday*) and subsequently embodied in a series of teaching tools.

6. Hirsch specifically noted that this core, the core of essential doctrines as viewed relatively consistently by the church over an extended time, can easily be contained in a relatively short paragraph.

Chapter 8: Moving beyond the Sacred/Secular Distinction

1. The church I attend in Lexington, Kentucky, once housed a porn theater. What better example of God's transforming power infiltrating and transforming a place?

2. For example, The Tribe's congregation in Los Angeles.

3. For example, the downtown campus of Embrace Church in Lexington.

4. For example, the initial building of Woodland Hills in St. Paul.

5. As usual, different translations choose different words here. Sometimes, the text is translated to reflect that God sent Christ while we were "hostile" or "weak" or "helpless." The point is, though, God did not wait for us to take the first step. God engaged first in mission to us.

6. Just for clarity, Deb and Al Hirsch are a husband and wife team engaged in the missional church movement.

7. There are, of course, counter-balancing factors that one always has to consider. For example, if my student had been an alcoholic in the past, I would have strongly discouraged him from taking on a project like this, one that would have exposed him to the possibility of relapse. But, there are all kinds of places into which we can carry the divine presence, places that will allow us to serve as

instruments in God's transformative work without exposing ourselves to past problems.

Chapter 9: Go and Make *Disciples!*

1. For those of you who want to go into more detail on this issue, with a particular focus on the early church period, see my *The Right Church: Living Like the First Christians* (Nashville: Abingdon, 2012).

2. In what follows, I am indebted to N. T. Wright's *Matthew for Everyone Part 2: Chapters 16–28* (Louisville: Westminster John Knox, 2004).

3. Mark 9:24.

4. Wright, *Matthew for Everyone*, 206.

5. In what follows I am indebted for certain insights to the *Theological Dictionary of the New Testament*, ed. Gerhard Kittel and Gerhard Friedrich, trans. G. W. Bromiley (Grand Rapids: Eerdmans, 1967). In particular, vol. IV, pages 416–61.

6. Ibid., 448.

7. Ibid., 449.

8. This invites all manner of discussions over details regarding beliefs, but that debate is not significant for the point I am making here.

9. This is expressed somewhat more clearly in the interaction between Jesus and Peter in the Gospel of John, though we want to be careful not too quickly to import John's somewhat different narrative into Matthew's account.

10. Mike Slaughter, interview by author, April 2012.

Chapter 10: Using All the Tools

1. I frequently teach seminary-level courses online for theological seminaries, and using YouTube for weekly lectures is a snap.

2. I list these three, as they are the three most popular in the United States. If you were to travel, say to China, you would have to take time to determine the relevant sites for that particular locale.

ABOUT THE AUTHOR

Dr. Charles (Chuck) Gutenson is a church consultant and former Chief Operating Officer of Sojourners. He previously served ten years at Asbury Seminary in Kentucky, most recently as the professor of Theology and Philosophy. He received an M.Div. from Asbury in 1995 and a Ph.D. in Philosophical Theology from Southern Methodist University in 2000. A member of the International Society of Theta Phi, an honor society for theological students, scholars in the field of religion and outstanding religious leaders, Chuck is the author of *The Right Church: Live Like the First Christians* and co-author, with Mike Slaughter, of *Hijacked: Responding to the Partisan Church Divide* and numerous articles on a variety of theological and philosophical issues.